NLP

D0754847

NLP

Revised edition

What the most successful people know, do and say

David Molden and Pat Hutchinson

Harlow, England • London • New York • Boston • San Francisco • Toronto • Sydney • Singapore • Hong Kong
Tokyo • Seoul • Taipei • New Delhi • Cape Town • Madrid • Mexico City • Amsterdam • Munich • Paris • Milan

PEARSON EDUCATION LIMITED
Edinburgh Gate
Harlow CM20 2JE
Tel: +44 (0)1279 623623
Fax: +44 (0)1279 431059
Website: www.pearsoned.co.uk

First published 2006
Revised edition published in Great Britain 2008

© Pearson Education Ltd 2008

ISBN 978-0-273-71493-4

British Library Cataloguing-in-Publication Data
A catalogue record for this book is available from the British Library.

Library of Congress Cataloging-in-Publication Data
A catalog record for this book is available from the Library of Congress.

10 9 8 7 6 5 4 3 2 1
11 10 09 08 07

Designed by Sue Lamble
Cartoon illustrations by Bill Piggins
Typeset in 10 pt Plantin by 3
Printed and bound in Great Britain by Clays Ltd., Bungay Suffolk

The Publisher's policy is to use paper manufactured from sustainable forests.

About the authors

David Molden is a personal development trainer and coach. As an NLP trainer since 1995, he has many years of experience working with people from all walks of life, including entrepreneurs, managers, sports professionals and children, in their ongoing pursuit of personal success.

David has a zest for life and an unremitting sense of fun. He maintains a high level of fitness and mind–body balance by training in kung fu and t'ai chi and has an interest in ancient wisdom and its relevance to today's society.

David is a director at Quadrant 1 International, a training and development company. He has appeared on TV and radio and is the author of several other books, including *Managing with the Power of NLP*, *NLP Business Masterclass* and *Beat Your Goals*.

Pat Hutchinson has a rich background of experience as an entrepreneur and leader of sales and marketing teams. She is an NLP trainer and a director at Quadrant 1 International.

Pat's combination of leading-edge personal change skills with a sense of practicality makes learning and applying NLP easy and enjoyable. Her ability to focus and get straight to the heart of the matter makes her a highly sought after trainer and coach. She has an enviable record of results with both individuals and business groups.

Both David and Pat can be contacted at:
success@quadrant1.com

Contents

Acknowledgements

We would like to thank all the people who have helped and supported us in the writing of this book – friends, family and the publishing team at Pearson Education. There are many more who made this book possible – all the people mentioned in this book whose names we have changed and who have achieved such great things with NLP. Our intention is that you will join them by having wonderful experiences in your life through the power of NLP.

Introduction

NLP can change your life. It is a remarkable force for change. We know this because we've seen it happen with many, many people over many years.

As a result of using NLP, we've seen people bring their dreams to life and make huge things happen – career and life crises solved, managers bringing about radical change in their companies, couples finding happiness after realising what is really important to them, teachers finding new ways to motivate children to learn, entrepreneurs operating at world-class levels, people changing the way they are perceived by others. In short, we've watched people use what they've learned to become more successful in everything they do. These people are the reason we know that NLP is *brilliant* – it has given so many the tools and techniques that have enabled them to take huge strides forward in their personal and professional lives, and you can join them.

> we've seen people bring their dreams to life and make huge things happen

What is NLP and what can it do for me?

NLP is a set of tools and techniques to help you deal with unhelpful patterns of thought and behaviour (some you won't even know you have) and introduce new, positive and constructive ways to improve your life. Although there are many tools and techniques in NLP, you don't need to learn them all to get started and *gain immediate benefit*. You can make amazing changes by using just one technique – simply use the exercises to experience what NLP has to offer and prepare to be astounded by the results.

A bit of history

NLP was created by Dr Richard Bandler and Dr John Grinder in the early 1970s in California. Bandler and Grinder have long since gone their separate ways, but have continued to develop NLP models and techniques. In the last 30 years or so, many others have contributed to this evolving field of personal change – too many to mention here. Our recent contribution can be found in the development of 'this not that' thinking in the section on reframing at the end of Chapter 3, and some of the exercises in Chapter 10. Bandler and Grinder wanted to discover how successful people achieve their results and then learn how to replicate their models. They began by modelling highly effective therapists but moved on to sales executives, negotiators, public speakers, trainers and leaders. Very soon they had drawn together the very best personal change tools from a variety of disciplines, plus models of excellence from their early subjects, and they designed the very first public training in NLP. Today NLP offers a vast array of effective tools and techniques for positive influence and change.

> NLP offers effective tools and techniques for positive influence and change

It does what it says on the tin

The letters 'NLP' stand for neurolinguistic programming. If you break down the name, it helps explain what it's all about:

- 'neuro' refers to the brain and nervous system
- 'linguistic' is the verbal and non-verbal language used to communicate
- 'programming' is the unique way you put all this together to create your behaviour.

You have one brain but two minds – one conscious and the other unconscious. When you get out of bed in the morning you begin running programmes stored in the depths of your unconscious mind – the one that remembers how to do all the things you do automatically: how to ride a bicycle, drive a car, make yourself feel good and make yourself feel bad. This storage area is much larger than the conscious mind you are using to read this book right now. The two minds work in a cooperative way – a typical example being when you are reading and your conscious mind suddenly switches to something else. Then, your unconscious mind takes over the reading and you arrive at the foot of the page not remembering anything about what you have just read.

Once formed, a programme has the capacity for amazing consistency, producing the same results over and over again. Some programmes will work well for you, while others may have undesirable results and be holding you back. NLP is used to change the programmes that are not working and create new ones that do.

For most people, things happen and they react. NLP offers a better way. It gives you the tools to react differently by choice and be more aware of your thoughts, feelings and behaviour. You will discover what really makes you tick and begin to make crystal clear decisions about what you want from work and life. Only you can take responsibility for your results and make changes to improve the quality of your life. It's like taking firm hold of the steering wheel used to direct your career and personal life and making it go where you decide, with a real sense of vision and determination. Once you have grasped it, you can use it to generate brilliant results in all areas of your life.

How well do you know yourself?

Have you ever wondered how it is that two people facing the same set of circumstances can produce diametrically opposite results? Why do some people achieve infinitely more than others? You may also have noticed how some people have a tendency to attract lively, vibrant people, while others are very good at attracting moaners and groaners. There are people who seem to have life sorted out just the way they want it and others who are either just surviving or struggling with frequent problems and difficulties. So what makes the difference?

Successful people are often thought of as lucky, but is it really luck? Luck infers that there is some form of gambling involved, but on close inspection these people show few signs of taking chances with their lives. Anyway, the sheer consistency with which they achieve good results defies the laws of gambling. No, it has more to do with **the way they think**. Taking control of your thinking is key in the pursuit of success. To do this, you first need to realise the impact your thinking is having on your life. You may think that circumstances beyond your control are keeping you where you are, like a frog in a well who thinks that the small circle of blue sky above is all there is outside the well. Not until he clings to the bucket for the journey skywards does he realise how much more there is out there. The techniques used in NLP are designed to increase your awareness and, as a consequence, your choices in life.

> Successful people are often thought of as lucky, but is it really luck?

New edition extras

We have received many e-mails from people who have read, enjoyed and benefited from the first edition of *Brilliant NLP*. They told us how much the examples and exercises helped them to apply NLP personally, overcome what they thought were limitations and create more of what they wanted out of life. We continue to be delighted and often amazed at the achievements of our readers and so, in this new edition, we have included more brilliant examples and additional techniques in Chapter 10. All the examples used are real, but we have changed the names to protect the confidentiality of the people involved. We have also introduced a brilliant tip at the end of each chapter to give you a little extra to work with. We trust that you will find the additional material useful and encourage you to e-mail us with your own examples of applying *Brilliant NLP* in your life.

Enjoy!

CHAPTER 1

Think your way to success

I magine your mind is like a kaleidoscope that has been left to form its own patterns over the years. Sometimes it falls one way and a pattern forms. Some time later, the kaleidoscope is knocked and it rolls into a different position, so the pattern changes and settles there for a while. Maybe this continues for a number of years until, one day, you decide to pick up the kaleidoscope and take control of the patternmaking. With one small twist, the whole colour scheme changes and forms a completely new and more exciting pattern. Twist again and another one appears and so on. The real challenge now is to decide which of the patterns is the most beautiful or, in terms of thought patterns, the most useful, empowering and enabling. So what is inside the kaleidoscope that makes up so many different patterns?

What are you storing in your unconscious mind and how useful is it?

Your patterns, in the kaleidoscope, represent how you think about yourself and your experiences, including:

- values
  - what's important to you personally
  - the value you place on people, things, places, activities and information
  - your intrinsic values (also called metaprogrammes)

- beliefs
    - what you believe about yourself and others
    - your opinions, judgements and capacity for conjecture.

What is important to you?

What is really important in your life? How about your work? What is it about your work that makes all the effort you put in worthwhile? What's important about your relationships with your partner, your immediate and extended family, friends and colleagues? When you ask these questions of yourself, where do your answers come from? Do they come from your head or your heart? These are your values – the things in life that are really important to you and you will go out of your way to protect, uphold and defend.

So do you know, with conviction, what is important to you? Does the tone of voice in which you answer these questions match the words you use to describe what is important or does it suggest that what you consider to be important to you is really an obligation? There is a big difference between a value born out of obligation and one born out of choice. This is a question you probably ask yourself rarely, yet the answer provides an insight into why you may be dissatisfied with certain areas of your life. You may think that the way to a fulfilled career and life is to set goals, make a plan and get on with it. If it were really that easy, wouldn't everyone be doing it?

> while you are busy the important things and people can get lost

Many of the things that are important to you are not even in your conscious awareness. They are not so easily rationalised and, while you are busy chasing a career, money, partner, happiness or some kind of recognition, the important things and people can get lost. What's important to you has a big impact on the way you behave. So if you feel that circumstances are forcing you to do things that go against your values, then you will feel an uncomfortable tug somewhere in your body. You may not know where it comes from, what is causing it or even what it is about. Such tugs appear in many different forms – it could be a feeling of discomfort, a fleeting thought or unpleasant memory or a shiver. The chances are that you will ignore them and move

> it makes sense to pay attention to tugs

on, but this is your unconscious mind giving you a signal that something demands your attention. You can ignore it, but, if you continue to do so, then you are suppressing the real you and your inherent energy. When energy becomes blocked, it can ultimately cause illness and disease. It makes sense to pay attention to tugs.

Where do your values come from?

You will have gathered values all your life, starting from the day you were born, and will have carried some of them with you into adulthood. What are they? How did you get them? What influence are they having on you?

- **Inherited values** are possibly the most common. As a child you will have been influenced by what was important to your parents, siblings, extended family, teachers and group leaders. Later on you will have become a little more selective, adapting the values of your chosen heroes from the worlds of sport, fashion, film, music, politics and so on. By the time you reached adulthood your values were already forming a major part of your adult programmes. For example, if you were always told to finish your food at mealtimes, you may now be eating much more than you need. If your parents were very academic, you may put a high value on acquiring formal qualifications.

- **Compensatory values** are formed when you go to an opposite extreme to compensate for something that didn't happen for you. For example, if you had a deprived childhood, you may compensate for that by overindulging your own children.

- **Your own judgements** or the way you perceive your own experiences will have an impact on the value you place on them. If you have ever been burgled or robbed, you are likely to place a high value on security, which may not be appropriate in some circumstances.

On the surface these values may seem innocent enough. However, on closer inspection it is surprising what a major role they play in determining the way your life pans out. When you recognise an uncomfortable tug, a feeling that all is not well, examine your values to determine whether or not what you are doing is violating a deeply held value. Use the following technique to discover your true values and make choices that will serve you well.

Discover your true values

Step 1

Think back to a time when you last felt a tug – was it to do with a relationship, your work, your family, your finances or your self-esteem and confidence? Then answer these questions.

- What is important to me about ....? (Complete with the subject of your tug.)

- What else is important to me about ....?

For example, you might start with 'What is important to me about my job?' and follow up with 'What else is important to me about my job?'

Continue asking this second question, making a list of your answers until you have all the possible answers. Then summarise the list and ask the question again. The thing *most* important to you may be so ingrained that you may not get to it until you have dug very deep indeed. You might list up to eight values, if not more.

In our example, you might get results such as, 'It's important that I am appreciated and valued at work', 'It's important that I am well paid' and 'It's important that my job has meaning – that it improves the world somehow.'

Step 2

Now, to find out what really is most important to you, take the value at the top of your list and compare it with each of the others in turn, asking, 'Which is more important?' Be firm and don't let yourself off the hook. Do this for each value in the list. You will end up with with a hierarchy of values in relation to your chosen area.

Step 3

Now examine your top three values, one at a time, and form a view on whether what you are doing is expressing or violating these values. For example, if in your relationship with your children you place a high value on trust, but you find yourself checking where they are and what time they are coming home, then your behaviour is conflicting with your value. At this point you have a choice as to whether to keep the value and change the behaviour or vice versa. Other values will be driving some of your behaviour, so it is important to remember that the object of this exercise is to gain clarity about your true values and the connection with your behaviour as this will help you to make decisions that serve you well. The intention is not to determine your number one value.

If your values are being violated, what are you going to do about it? Can you change your behaviour to bring it into line with your values? Maybe one (or more) of your values is no longer valid and you have been hanging on to it as a result of habit – where

> If your values are being violated, what are you going to do about it?

did it come from? Is it a value that works for you in some circumstances but not others? Can you change this value? Do you know someone with different values in this area? What would happen if you changed it? How would things be different for you? Asking these questions is the first step towards creating change.

Intrinsic values

So far, we have looked at the values you have accumulated as a result of your life experiences. Underlying these are some deeper-rooted values that determine the way you approach life. They are called metaprogrammes – the source of your core motivation and behaviour patterns.

Intrinsic values are easily recognisable because they show themselves as patterns in what you say, how you say it and what you do. The key here is not deciding whether the behaviour is right or wrong but whether it is useful in the circumstances.

Think of these programmes on a continuum, with 0 and 10 representing the extremes. You might function at one point on the continuum at work and at another in your personal life. There is no right or wrong – it is a question of whether or not it is useful in any given context. You will recognise yourself as we describe the extremes at each end of the continuum.

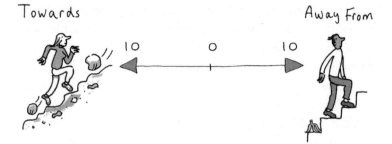

Towards   Away From   10   0   10

The towards and away from programmes

If you have a *towards* programme, you are recognisable by your drive. You set goals easily and are frequently creating new goals for yourself. Sometimes you disregard the risks involved and, at the extreme end, may not complete one goal before beginning another.

● Advantages – forward-thinking, goal-orientated, positive energy and drive.

● Disadvantages – may get entangled in too many new initiatives at once, may be perceived as gung-ho and have a tendency to leave things unfinished.

If you have an *away from* programme, you focus on avoiding risks and making sure everything is safe before moving forward. You sometimes miss out on life and work experiences as a result of fear of taking a risk. Typical behaviour includes being over-insured 'just in case' and, when asked what you want, you reply with a list of things you don't want. You hold back from getting involved in anything new until all concerns have been fully addressed. You put a high priority on all forms of security.

● Advantages – very good at assessing risks and recognising what to avoid.

● Disadvantages – overly cautious, with a tendency to focus on the downside, may appear negative and unwilling to try new experiences, and make choices based on avoidance rather than a desire for something new.

The options and procedures programmes

If you have an *options* programme, you like to have choice in your life – considering different makes and models when buying a car, different areas when buying a house and the many varieties of food on offer when going out for a meal, for example. At the extreme end, your behaviour can be perceived as procrastination, particularly to someone who values procedure. You have a tendency to keep going over and over choices, as if making a decision might cause regret later.

- Advantages – explores many options and provides people with choices; happy to test and break rules.
- Disadvantages – may procrastinate and avoid making decisions until forced to do so by circumstances; very good at reinventing the wheel.

In a *procedures* programme, you have schemes to follow in order to be effective. You become confused and frustrated when faced with too many options. You write lists, tick things off as you go and are very efficient at completing tasks that require an ordered sequence. You may, however, find it difficult to accept a new procedure, which is more than likely to have been written by an options-orientated person. In order to get involved in a creative thinking session, you need a procedure detailing how to do it.

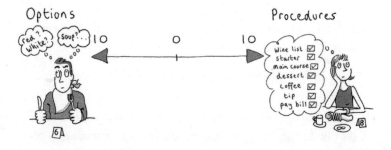

You require structure and clear processes for getting things done.

- Advantages – very efficient, good with rule-based administration and will stick to agreed rules.
- Disadvantages – the procedure may become more important than the job to be done; at worst, bureaucratic and blocking.

The in-time and thru-time programmes

You are *in-time* if you live 'in the moment', not worrying about what comes next – whether or not you are going to be late for your next meeting or arriving late at a party, if indeed you get there at all, for example. You give people your full attention because they are there with you now. You value each moment and are fully engaged with whatever you are doing at any time.

- Advantages – can concentrate on tasks; emotionally and mentally engaged in each and every experience.
- Disadvantages – frequently late and can give the impression of not being concerned about timekeeping; may get involved in too many things as a result of attachment.

If you spend your time planning and making sure that you are not late for meetings, parties and any other engagements, you have a *thru-time* pattern. This preoccupation with planning your next move or analysing the last may prevent you from concentrating on the matter in hand. Your thinking is constantly flitting

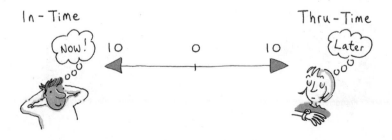

across past, present and future. You may appear to others to be disinterested.

- Advantages – good planner and timekeeper.
- Disadvantages – may give the impression of not being engaged in the current activity and being on time and scheduling activities can become more important than the activities themselves.

The internally and externally referenced programmes

The simplest way to think about our next pattern is in terms of how you measure yourself and how you evaluate situations. If you are *internally referenced,* you instinctively know when you have done a good job and will want to solve all your own problems. You rarely ask for advice from other people. You make decisions based on your own judgements, feelings and opinions. You don't need reassurance from other people. In fact, if you are given such reassurance, thanks or appreciation, you are likely to view it with suspicion. You will also know when you have done a job badly and this, again, will be judged against your own criteria rather than external evidence. You can appear aloof and insular and possibly overconfident to an externally referenced person.

- Advantages – can stay motivated when there is little feedback or praise.
- Disadvantages – internal standards may override, and

Internal Frame of Reference   External Frame of Reference sometimes cancel out, external evidence; will disregard evidence, facts and sound advice from other people.

If you are *externally referenced*, you measure yourself against the feedback from other people. You value this and will go out of your way to find it. To internally referenced people, you can appear needy and lacking in self-sufficiency. When faced with a challenge, you will seek facts, evidence, advice and opinions from other people and sources.

● Advantages – will make decisions based on concrete facts and evidence or maybe just the 'feel good' factor, so long as it comes from an external source; able to give excellent customer service and help to others.

● Disadvantages – will get stressed when there is a lack of external feedback. Needs frequent feedback on performance to make good progress; will be indecisive if there is a lack of feedback.

The self and others programmes

Who comes first – you or the team/family/group? If you have a *self* pattern, you speak in terms of 'I' and 'What's in it for me?' You believe that people are capable of looking after themselves. You help yourself to coffee, push in front of traffic queues, take the last chocolate and put yourself first when making decisions.

● Advantages – looks after self and is very self-sufficient; avoids getting tangled up in other people's problems.

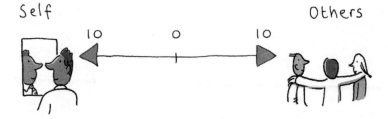

- Disadvantages – does not engender good team spirit
  and sometimes may be perceived as arrogant and/or
  uncaring.

With an *others* pattern, you spend a lot of time making sure
everyone is comfortable and happy and may neglect your own
needs and wants. You serve other people coffee and put yourself
last in the queue. You are a courteous driver and have a genuine
concern for the well-being of others. Your day-to-day decisions
are made taking account of other people, not wanting to cause
them upset or discomfort.

- Advantages – good team player, looking out for the needs of
  others; does well in caring professions.
- Disadvantages – personal well-being can suffer as a result of
  putting other people first; can be perceived as unpredictable
  because many decisions are based on what others think and
  how they might react; considers the welfare of the team to
  be more important than getting the job done.

The detail and global programmes

As a *detail* person, you will be concerned about the specifics of a
situation. Your conversations are likely to be long and drawn out
to cover all the details. Focusing on detail sometimes means you
forget the overall purpose.

- Advantages – very comfortable working with details and
  excellent at spotting small mistakes; copes very well with
  large documents and small print.

- Disadvantages – can get bogged down in detail and work away happily, even though the purpose may have changed; may be perceived as pedantic or fastidious.

If you have a *global* pattern, you look at situations from the bigger picture and speak in general terms, avoiding detail. You move conversations on to different topics in preference to discussing details. You may have little to say about some topics and may frequently need to be brought back to the point.

- Advantages – makes a good strategist or concept creator; can generate big ideas.

- Disadvantages – may appear to have your head in the clouds; may feel uncomfortable holding a detailed conversation; frustration with details may result in too many ideas and little execution.

▶ brilliant example

Kim has an *options* and *global* pattern. She experienced feelings of inadequacy when her partner, who had a *detail* and *procedures* pattern, was able to book the family holiday efficiently, taking care of all the details. He would spend time studying brochures and, by a process of elimination, decide on the right one and book it, apparently without any feelings of stress. When Kim tried to do the same, she became distracted and overwhelmed by all the different choices. The reason for her frustration came from her preference for thinking *globally* and keeping her *options* open. Once she realised this, she was able to relax, laugh at herself and allow her partner to do what he is good at.

The feeling and thinking programmes

With a *feeling* pattern, you react emotionally to a variety of situations and rely on your intuition or 'gut feeling' to make decisions. You are emotionally engaged with all life experiences.

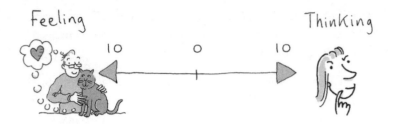

- Advantages – takes people's feelings into account when making decisions.
- Disadvantages – can appear emotive; others may be wary of evoking an emotional response.

As someone with a *thinking* pattern, you take a pragmatic and logical approach to situations while remaining emotionally detached.

- Advantages – decisions are made based on logic, fact and evaluation.
- Disadvantages – can appear to be cold and unfeeling; may not consider the feelings of others before speaking and acting.

The sameness and difference programmes

As someone with an extreme *sameness* pattern, you will probably visit the same place on holiday every year, take the same route to work each day, sit at your favourite spot in your favourite restaurant, eating the same food as you always do on the same night each week. When approaching something new, you will generate understanding by looking for similarities with previous experiences. Repetition doesn't bore you – it instils comfort and familiarity. You are likely to remain in the same job for many years.

- Advantages – can be relied on to complete repetitive activities successfully.

- Disadvantages – may be perceived as unadventurous by others; may not be willing to try new things, even if they could be beneficial.

With an extreme *difference* pattern, you are likely to be constantly on the lookout for new things to do or new ways of doing current things. You rarely go back to the same place twice, always wanting to try new foods in new restaurants and new locations for holidays. You get bored easily and may find yourself changing jobs frequently due to a need for difference.

- Advantages – happy to try out new ideas and concepts; gains many different life experiences.

- Disadvantages – sometimes creates change for the sake of creating change; doesn't understand the concept of 'if it works, don't fix it'; lack of stability.

brilliant example

Martin realised that he had a strong *difference* pattern and, every few months, he would become bored with his job and seek a change. Realising that this was not a recipe for success, he decided to accommodate his difference pattern **within** his role, and social life, and still be able to progress successfully at work. When the tugs of familiarity occurred, he could recognise them quickly and deal with them.

Using what you've learned about your programmes

By now, you will have an idea of your intrinsic values. With some, you will already have the flexibility to be able to operate at either end of the continuum. If you operate mainly from one end, you might reap the benefits in some situations, but you will also feel the effects of the disadvantages in others. If you can develop flexibility over all the programmes, you will have the advantages with none of the disadvantages.

> mismatching of intrinsic values is a very common cause of misunderstanding, stress and conflict

Mismatching of intrinsic values is a very common cause of misunderstanding, stress and conflict in life. When people speak of a 'personality clash', it is invariably a mismatch of values or misunderstanding of metaprogrammes.

For example, many relationships break down because of a mismatch of the *in-time/thru-time* programmes. As one partner is ready and waiting to set off to go out for a meal with friends, for example, the other is still chatting on the telephone, showing no sense of urgency. The *thru-time* person feels devalued and frustrated, while the *in-time* person wonders what all the fuss is about. It's the repetition and interplay of these patterns that eventually causes a relationship to break down.

Similarly, you can bore a *global* thinker rigid if you give too much detail about your journey to work or the state of your health or what little Suzie got up to in the bath last night. Someone who places a high value on choice is going to feel frustrated if asked to follow a five-step plan, while a person who is always late and unprepared will irritate someone who values planning. Combinations of profiles can produce different behavioural patterns in different people. Mismatching of programmes in job profiles is a common cause of stress in the workplace.

These programmes are unconscious so, when you become involved in activities that go against them, you feel that uncomfortable tug. You may even say to yourself something like:

- 'Why am I always late for meetings?'
- 'Why is it that Sally and Paul always manage to book their holiday well in advance and I'm still messing around with the brochures while they are jetting off?'
- 'I hate my job, but I'll stay because I'm not sure if I would enjoy a new one.'
- 'Why do I never finish anything before I start something new?'
- 'I never seem to make up my mind to do anything.'
- 'It doesn't matter how hard I work, my manager never seems to appreciate me.'

Are your intrinsic values holding you back?

The examples given above demonstrate conflicts of intrinsic values, each having advantages and disadvantages. They indicate a lack of flexibility due to being 'stuck' at one end of a continuum. Here's an exercise to help you identify any patterns that may be the cause of conflict for you.

Identifying a conflict caused by an intrinsic value

Step 1

From the programme descriptions, choose those for which you consider yourself to be predominantly at one end of the continuum. Write the name of the programmes below.

Programme: _____

Programme: _____

Programme: _____

Step 2

Pick a situation where you have experienced conflict with another person or frustration with a task or responsibility.

Situation: _____

Step 3

Consider the role that you have been playing in this situation and ask yourself which of the programmes you identified in Step 1 is responsible for the conflict. Imagine how it might change if you were to function from the opposite end of the offending continuum. Take your time to think this through carefully. Acting so differently may feel awkward, but this is merely a sign that you have begun to develop your behavioural flexibility.

How you respond to experiences will depend on the nature of your values. If you once trusted someone and were let down, there are a number of ways in which you could respond. You may decide never to trust anyone again or you may decide that any future trust will have conditions attached. Alternatively, you may retain your belief in trusting and hope that one day this person will also realise that. Each of these reactions has a very different underpinning value that results from the meaning you have accrued from your life experiences.

Adapting your intrinsic values to give you more choice

An awareness of your intrinsic values is very often enough to create change. Sometimes, however, awareness is not enough and circumstances may suggest that a change in behaviour could be beneficial. As the majority of behaviour is habitual, the challenge lies in breaking the old habits and developing new ones by repetition.

brilliant example

Gary had an *away from* and *external reference* pattern and had spent a good many years making decisions based on what he wanted to avoid (away from motivation). This, coupled with his external reference pattern, caused him to be very uncertain about his own choices. Gary chose his current job 15 years ago not because he wanted it, but to avoid the insecurity of being jobless. This one decision led him to spend 15 years in a job he dislikes, surviving by avoiding any situation that he found awkward or uncomfortable, including meetings with other managers.

Gary's very powerful habit of both avoiding difficult situations and not knowing how to make good decisions brought with it a great deal of stress. Having been given a little help to change the habit, he is now pursuing a more fulfilling and engaging endeavour and looking a good deal younger and healthier as a result.

If you have developed a strong habit of behaving in a certain way, it may seem very odd to begin acting the opposite way by, for example, introducing difference when you are not used to change. You may not know how to act differently and find the change awkward and unnatural. This in itself will create a tug for you – a feeling that something isn't right – and you may want to revert to your more usual behaviour. If this happens, remind yourself why you want to change and that the tug will diminish the more you repeat the new behaviour. Think of the tug as a signal that you are making a transition from old habit to new and that this will help you to become more flexible as a person.

brilliant tip

Listen to your language, particularly your use of words like *must*, *should* and *need*. Are these words limiting you in any way? Are the things you consider important really so important? What if you were to relax your own rules attached to *must*, *should* and *need*? What new possibilities might be created by dropping your insistence on having things a certain way? Develop a new habit by means of repetition. The more often you act in a different way, the sooner the new habit will develop. Observe someone you admire for the way they act and adopt their approach. Notice what they do and listen to the language they use. This will save you from having to work it *all* out for yourself.

CHAPTER 2

Don't believe everything you hear!

Your beliefs are connected to your values and are very personal. They form a significant part of the pattern in your personal kaleidoscope. If you value trust, you are likely to hold beliefs such as:

- people can be trusted
- there is no need for rules
- people can manage their own schedules and productivity
- my children will come home when they say they will.

If you place a high value on mistrust, you are likely to believe the opposite:

- only fools trust others
- people are out to get me
- I have to watch what you are doing because you can't be trusted
- I have to phone my children when it's time for them to come home.

The beliefs expressed above probably came from experience and it's amazing how little you need to form a belief. How many times does Johnny have to be late home from school before Mum develops a habit of reminding him to come straight home because she has formed the belief that 'Johnny is always late home from school'? How many times do you have to be ignored by someone for you to formulate the belief that he or she is uncaring or arrogant? We're not saying that all beliefs are wrong or inappropriate, but, rather, that it is good to test them to see if they are acting as a barrier or limitation. Once you have formed a belief, it can become self-fulfilling in that others behave in a way that is expected of them. For example, if Johnny believes that Mum anticipates him being late, then he will develop

> it's amazing how little you need to form a belief

the habit. If you regularly tell Johnny that he is lazy, he will prove you right. Holding a limiting belief is like wearing blinkers – you see only what you expect to see and block out counter-evidence. Because your beliefs are personal, you will defend them and seek evidence to justify them. This is fine if the belief is positive, such as 'Johnny has potential that is worth developing', but consider the consequences of believing 'Johnny will never make the grade'.

Are you being held back by limiting beliefs?

So who is turning the kaleidoscope of your mind? Who is imposing their limiting beliefs on you? The people around you will undoubtedly have a hand in making small turns, changing your beliefs and having an impact on your behaviour.

brilliant example

A mother and daughter attended the same training course. About to embark on a physical activity, the mother turned to her daughter and said, 'You'll never be able to do that, you aren't coordinated.'

Fortunately the facilitator overheard the comment and the girl was asked to walk across the room. She did so elegantly, proving that she was indeed coordinated. Imagine being continually told that you are not coordinated. What kind of limitation would that put on you? How long is the list of activities you would go out of your way to avoid?

Think back to your schooldays. How many things did you do poorly or drop out of because you believed that you couldn't do them? Did your teachers, parents or peers reinforce or help you to create any limiting beliefs? Take a few moments to think of all the things that you could have been doing now if you hadn't carried these limiting beliefs to the present day.

At work, how many people are being held back by the limiting beliefs of their managers? In our workshops, we find an astonishingly high number. Many managers don't delegate, encourage, stretch or even recognise superb performance in their people. One reason for this is their belief in their own capability as a manager and another is their beliefs about the capabilities of others. Helping teams to develop positive beliefs and values about colleagues can dramatically change attitudes, which quickly cascade through the company, with subsequent improvement in performance. If you can identify and change a limiting belief, you can make huge strides forward.

> if you can identify and change a limiting belief, you can make huge strides forward

A single belief represents just a small part of the kaleidoscope pattern and is often itself part of a cluster of similar beliefs. In the extreme, a cluster of limiting beliefs can lead into a whole host of unpleasant areas, including phobias, blaming others, anger and low self-esteem. Being in control of your own kaleidoscope, therefore, is key to your success. The simple demonstration in our brilliant example created an awareness for the daughter that completely changed her beliefs about what coordination means. She went on to complete the exercise and learned to juggle three balls in under ten minutes.

Beliefs can be either limiting or empowering. Are yours serving you well? How can you recognise them and what can you do about them? Let's look at how to challenge limiting beliefs that may be hindering you.

A hard-working woman recently presented us with the belief 'you have to work to earn money'. It was attached to a value about having enough money for her family to be secure. It was also important for her to have an active social life and spend time with her family. However, she had developed the habit of working late and at weekends. She became increasingly unhappy.

When she realised that the belief was causing stress, she let go of it. She continued to enjoy her job as well as spending time going to concerts with friends and being with her family. Very quickly her new, and more powerful, belief became 'enjoying time with friends will give me the fulfilment that I am seeking'. This attracted a whole new set of beliefs about what she was and wasn't going to do. The initial change to her work belief triggered a series of belief changes, much like a falling stack of cards.

How do you recognise a limiting belief?

This may seem like a simple change, but beliefs can be stubborn, defying the most rigorous logic. First, you need to know how to identify a limiting belief from what people say. A limiting belief is a simple statement that will usually begin with one of the following.

- 'I can't . . .'
- 'People should . . .'
- 'They don't want . . .'
- 'Everyone/no one thinks . . .'

Here are a few classic examples.

- 'I can't maintain a long-term relationship.'
- 'People never listen to me.'

- 'He is easily distracted.'
- 'Learning a foreign language is difficult.'
- 'I'm no good at maths.'

Here's a simple belief changing exercise.

Shaking unhelpful beliefs

Whenever you hear yourself making the kind of statement mentioned above, use this exercise. There are three steps to take to change an unhelpful belief.

Step 1

Shake its roots by challenging it. Answer the following questions.

- Have I always believed this?
- Where did this belief come from?
- Is the belief still valid?
- What evidence do I have to support the belief?
- Who do I know who holds an opposite belief?
- What evidence suggests that the belief is untrue?
- In what way is the belief absurd or ridiculous?

Step 2

Find an alternative, more empowering belief – brainstorm for beliefs that open up more possibilities. This is a matter of 'trying on' a variety of beliefs until you find one that fits. Make sure that your new belief is stated in the positive – for example, 'I can learn a foreign language and I am learning something new in each lesson.'

Step 3

Integrate the alternative belief. Imagine how things will be different and gauge how you feel about this change. Imagine yourself doing what you will be doing as a result. Imagine having a conversation holding your new belief. Is this motivating you? Does it feel good? If necessary, try on another belief and go through the same process. Then select the belief(s) that make you feel really good about yourself. Before finally committing to the new belief, consider how it might affect other people.

Congratulate yourself for having taken control of your kaleidoscope. You have rid yourself of a limiting belief and created another that is infinitely more powerful. Even better is that, over time, this new way of thinking will become a habit and you will generate empowering beliefs naturally.

brilliant tip

Think of your beliefs and values as a tree. The values form the stable trunk and the beliefs are the fruit. Sometimes the fruit is fresh and bright and nutritious, sometimes it rots and falls off the tree and is no longer appetising. Every now and again, it's worth giving the branches a good shake so that old and unwanted beliefs fall to the ground.

CHAPTER 3

Think your way to feeling great

When you feel anxious, uncertain, confused, angry or frustrated, you become tense and stressed. This will prevent you from accessing all your wonderful inner resources. Whatever situation you are in, if you are feeling any of these, it is unlikely that you are performing to your full potential. Think of a time recently when you were feeling stressed and recall what was on your mind. Your thoughts were responsible for creating your feelings. Every thought you have results in a feeling, so the way to control your feelings is to control your thoughts.

Test this out. Sit quietly and think of a situation when you did something that you didn't feel so good about. Notice what feelings come up. Now take a deep breath and think about a situation where you did something that you felt really good about and, again, notice the feelings that come up.

You have just used your imagination to recall two experiences that resulted in very different feelings. You can use the connection between your imagination and your feelings to put you in control

> you can use the connection between your imagination and your feelings to put you in control

and enable you to choose the way you feel. Your feelings have a direct impact on your capability, regardless of the situation.

It's the first thought that counts

Everything begins with a thought and that thought will attract similar ones until you have a cluster of thoughts. That cluster becomes a pattern of thinking, which forms a habit. The habit will then be applied to many different scenarios. Scientists believe that the conscious mind is able to cope with only about seven pieces of information at any one time and can become overloaded very quickly. This means that, if you fill your conscious mind with negative thought patterns that create negative feelings, you have no room for anything else. By taking control, you are exercising more choice over your conscious thinking and the more you do this, the more you will build a reserve of unconscious patterns that work effectively for you.

The first step in taking control is to be aware of how thoughts are generated. When you think, you have an internal selection process. If you were to absorb everything happening around you, your brain would become overloaded, so you select what you consider to be important and ignore the rest. For example, think about a conversation you had recently or a television programme you watched – how much do you remember? Chances are, you will be able to summarise the event and expand on the aspects of most interest to you, but you won't be able to recall every word. Your internal selection process has chosen what it wants to retain as a combination of images and sounds with the feelings you had at the time. Added to this will be some internal dialogue – in other words, what you have said to yourself about the situation.

This is how you represent your unique version of reality – in pictures, sounds, internal dialogue and feelings, as well as, sometimes, smell and taste. You capture your personal understanding of reality via a combination of your external senses and inner thoughts and it is this captured version that you use to make decisions and form judgements. This unique perspective of events is called your 'internal representation' or 'map of reality'.

Let's take a look at these components of your internal representation, beginning with the visual sense.

Working with your visual imagery

Bring to mind a pleasant memory and spend a few moments enjoying it. Capture the imagery, then come back to the book when you are ready.

Describe the image you created? Was it clear? Was it in colour? Did it have a frame around it or did the edges fade away? Did it have depth? Was there any movement? Was it bright or dark and murky? How about the contrast and detail? How close was this image to you and did you project it above or below the horizon? Could you see yourself in the image or was the image all around you?

Just as you can look at the visual details of a photograph or a movie, you can look at the details of the images that make up your thoughts. These details refer to the qualities of the image, but not the image itself. The ability to imagine and change these qualities is unlimited. The number of different qualities you can work with in your mental imagery will be determined by the amount of

> the ability to imagine and change these qualities is unlimited

practice you have had at doing so. Just as you intentionally imagined a pleasant experience, the very same process happens hundreds, if not thousands, of times each day to represent each thought you are having. Sometimes you may not be aware of your mental imagery, but it is there nonetheless and you can use it to good effect.

▶ **brilliant** **example**

Harriet was having difficulty leaving her work behind at the end of the day. She was becoming more and more stressed as the pile just didn't seem to go down.

During coaching, we acknowledged that Harriet was very fond of pretty things. We asked her to visualise herself at the end of the day wrapping the outstanding work up in pretty coloured paper, tying a coloured bow around it and leaving it there until the next morning when she could unwrap it and continue with her work. Harriet became much more relaxed about her work after that and her productivity increased.

Let's play around with your visual imagery a little and see how easy it is to change, or reprogramme, your thoughts and feelings.

Zap away bad feelings

It is quite easy to eliminate bad feelings for any situation in which you would like to feel more in control or be more confident. Perhaps the thought of facing a difficult situation with someone is causing you to feel frustrated, tense or low in confidence. At times like these, when you are emotionally stressed, you consume a great deal of energy making yourself feel bad. Even though you don't enjoy feeling bad, it may be something over which you have had no control in the past. When you are feeling this way, you have entered the realm of 'self-preservation'. As a result, your ability to think rationally and make sound decisions is impaired. The goal then becomes one of survival, saving face, winning or seeking recognition. You only have to feel that way once or twice before a habit, or programme, is formed and then you have set a pattern for thinking yourself into bad feelings. Eliminate the bad feelings by using the following technique.

Zapping away bad feelings

Bring to mind a specific time when you were unhappy with the way you felt or behaved. Now focus on the image that comes to mind as you first access the memory. Quickly send it zooming away into the distance. As it goes, notice that it gets smaller and smaller until it disappears completely. It's just like the starship *Enterprise* whizzing off at warp factor 10 into deep space and, in a fraction of a second, disappearing completely from view in an instant. You can do the same thing with all your images of unpleasant experiences – just zap them off into deep space. As you do, notice how much better you feel.

brilliant example

John had an *away from* pattern that was causing him a great deal of stress as he predicted all the awful things that might happen to him. He had plenty of time to dwell on these thoughts when walking his dog in the mornings. As he did so, his head would go down into the internal dialogue position as he told himself how awful things were.

During coaching, we suggested that, while out dog-walking, he might keep his head up and notice the scenery around him, visualising all the good things that had happened the day before.

Now exercise your ability to *choose* something *different* using the following technique.

Choosing to respond differently

As soon as you have zapped away the negative image using the technique described above, bring to mind a memory with positive feelings attached to it. It might be an experience where you were very confident or highly motivated to achieve a positive result.

Now work on the image. Make sure that it is colourful, big and bright.

When you have intensified these qualities, bring the image closer and imagine stepping into it. Take a few moments to absorb and enjoy the positive feelings generated by this effect.

Working with your internal audio

As well as making pictures in your mind, you can replay conversations with other people, environmental sounds and music. Do you sometimes replay conversations or anticipate a future event and actually hear what people said or might say? This internal audio may or may not be accompanied by images.

What about your internal dialogue? What do you find yourself saying over and over in your mind?

> your internal voice is very powerful and has a direct influence on how you feel

Your internal voice is very powerful and has a direct influence on how you feel at any particular moment in time. A great deal of your emotions are carried in the tone of your voice – both spoken words and those you say to yourself.

Here's something to think about. If you were to record all your internal dialogue for one day and then play it back, would it motivate you?

You can explore and change the qualities of your internal audio in much the same way as you did above with mental imagery. Use the following technique to change the way you feel when you think about a future event. It can be used in all kinds of situations when you want to feel a certain way. How do you want to feel when you wake up in the morning, when you get to work on Monday, when your partner does something that annoys you? How many different voices can you create for yourself?

Use your inner voice to change the way you feel

Think about an upcoming event that is important to you and decide how you want to feel at that time. Now choose an actor or someone you know well who has the tone of voice that you want to have at this event.

Imagine that the event is just about to start and have a conversation with yourself in the voice tone you have chosen. For example, you may want to feel confident and determined to get a result. Choose the voice of one of your heroes, saying, 'This is an important day for me. I will be asking some tough questions and expecting clear answers. I will be positive, focused and determined to get a result we can act on.' Now say it again and turn up the volume. Adjust the tone and pace until you begin to feel confident and determined.

You can also turn the volume down when your internal dialogue gets carried away with itself. When you keep repeating negative dialogue over and over, telling yourself what a mess you made of this or that or churning over a work problem when you are trying to sleep, simply turn the volume down and notice the words fading away into the distance until they have gone completely. You can also change negative voices into humorous voices, such as Bart Simpson or Mickey Mouse. Notice how easily the negative feelings disappear!

When you realise that you have control over your inner voice and associated sounds, you can walk around with a symphony orchestra in your head and a host of film stars and cartoons at the ready should you require their services. Have fun.

Feeling fantastic

The feelings you have during a day are the result of how you have chosen to associate with your experiences. This is the emotional domain. The word used to describe these feelings is 'kinaesthetic'.

Your feelings are generated from imagined events as well as real experiences. If you have an argument with a partner or a disagreement with a shop assistant, the feelings you have will be part of a learned pattern of reacting to those circumstances. A memory consists of visual, auditory and kinaesthetic elements, sometimes including smells and tastes as well. Feelings result from thinking in a particular way. For example, a feeling of apprehension may be the result of creating dark, murky images and internal dialogue that is warning you to be on the alert for an awkward or difficult situation. Imagine how this contrasts with the feelings of another person in the same situation who is creating bright, clear images with internal dialogue that is full of excitement.

You have the capacity for a wide range of feelings, from excited highs to heavy lows and, at worst, depression. There are many techniques to help you feel the way you want to feel. Some of them help you to change the feelings you have attached to negative memories, while others give you a way of creating any feeling you want at any time.

Use your best experiences to feel great

The way we attach feelings to our thoughts is very haphazard. We allow people and circumstances to influence the way we feel. Once a thought has a feeling attached, it becomes well and truly anchored. Each time we recall that thought, the exact same feeling will surface. For example, when you look at a photograph taken on a great holiday, the feelings you had at the time return. When you answer the phone and hear the voice of someone you had a negative experience with, you feel the same way as when that experience happened.

Anchored feelings become embedded in your memory very easily. A classic anchor is when you have a bad encounter with a sales assistant and decide never to visit that shop again. Whenever someone mentions the shop's name, you relive the feelings you had at the time of your encounter, even though it may have taken place a long time ago.

The process of anchoring feelings to thoughts is an automatic feature of the unconscious mind. The result is called a 'state' – not just a state of mind, but rather, a state of mind and body as the way you think and feel causes the body to become either relaxed or tense. Now, what if you could use this process to create great feelings, or states, whenever you wanted them? In other words, exercise choice over the feelings you anchor and the states you create. What if you could produce feelings of being courageous, confident, calm, decisive, optimistic, attentive, playful, empathetic, curious or focused? What if you could create a positive state for learning and being open-minded; for leadership, motherhood, fatherhood; for being dynamic or having abundant energy; for love, sensitivity? Well, you can with the following very simple technique.

▶ brilliant example

Louise had to present to the board of directors on a regular basis. The more she did it, the more nervous she became. On one particular day, she was excited that she was going to present her new idea, which would save the company a great deal of money. She was also anxious about blowing it and really wanted to get the board to listen to her idea.

We helped Louise to access a confident state she knew well from another situation and anchor this state to the boardroom door handle. As soon as she touched the handle, the confident state emerged and she was able to give her presentation.

Anchoring states you want

Decide which state you would like to anchor. Choose one from the list above or you may have some other specific state in mind. For the purpose of this exercise, we will call it 'state X'. Read through the exercise and commit it to memory – you will need to keep your attention focused internally throughout the process, so you will not want to be checking the book for what to do next!

Preparing for the exercise

You are going to attach a state to a trigger point somewhere on your body, such as pinching your ear or squeezing your thumb. Choose something that you are unlikely to do accidentally and can repeat with precision.

The procedure

1 Recall a time when you had a strong feeling of having state X and keep thinking about this memory. Choose any context you like, as long as the feeling of state X is very strong. If you can't think of one, then put yourself into an imaginary situation where you are in a high level of state X. Pay attention to the qualities of your image and any sounds. You are going to use this internal representation to intensify the feeling of state X. It may help to close your eyes as you do this exercise.

2 Project the image in front of you above the horizon level. Make sure you are looking at yourself in the image.

3 Put a frame around the image. Make it colourful and bright with a high level of contrast. If sound is involved, adjust an imaginary graphic equaliser so that it is across the full range of treble, middle and bass. Make it surround sound.

4 Intensify the colour, brightness, contrast and sound.

5 Slowly bring the image closer to you and notice how the frame eventually disappears until the image is so close that it has enveloped you and is all around you. As the feeling of state X

approaches the peak of its intensity, set your anchor by gently squeezing your thumb (or pinching your ear or whichever anchor you chose). Release the anchor as soon as the sensation begins to diminish.

Anchoring a positive state

6   Now take a couple of deep breaths to change your state. Wait a few moments and then trigger or fire your anchor! Enjoy the intensity of feeling state X. Fire it a few times more to get used to it and strengthen it. Make sure that you break your state by breathing deeply between each firing. Now you can use this anchor any time you want to have the feelings associated with state X.

You can test the anchor by future pacing. Think about a situation in the future where you will want state X. As you run through the scenario in your mind, fire your anchor. The key to successful anchoring is the intensity of feeling, the timing of setting the anchor and the precision in setting and firing the anchor.

Just as you can create a positive anchor, you can eliminate negative anchors. For example, you may have had a negative experience with someone in which you did not cope well. You may have had bad experiences at work that are still causing you to lose confidence or become frustrated. Your reaction in these situations creates a negative state that makes your inner resources inaccessible. Even though the incident might have happened some time ago, you still carry the feelings associated with it and behave accordingly. Your behaviour reinforces your state and forms a strong habit, such that, every time you find yourself in a similar situation, the limiting behaviour is triggered. The following technique uses space and physical location to relieve these negative and stressful feelings. You needn't keep those bad feelings in your memory – you can collapse them and, if you wish, replace them with positive feelings.

▶ brilliant example

Phil realised, with coaching, that he had deliberately been perpetuating a negative relationship with Sarah, his colleague. Whenever they met, he would be in a negative, defensive state, which Sarah would pick up on. They would argue and part feeling bad.

Using the collapsing anchors technique, below, Phil was able to establish a new way of approaching Sarah to rebuild the relationship.

Collapsing anchors

1   Mark two spaces on the floor about 2 metres (6 feet) apart.

2   Label one space with a minus sign, the other with a plus sign.

3   Stand on the minus sign and bring an unpleasant memory into your mind. Talk about the event for a minute or so and check how you feel as you recall the experience.

4   Take a couple of deep breaths and walk briskly over to the plus sign space, bringing a pleasant memory into your mind, making this more intense than the negative feeling. Talk about this

experience for a minute or so, paying attention to the images and sounds you use to recall the events. Intensify the qualities of colour, size, clarity, brightness and volume, then bring the image close to you. Bring the image closer and closer and notice how your feelings intensify. Hold this feeling for a few moments and then relax.

5 Staying on the plus sign, talk again about the earlier unpleasant experience and notice how the negative feelings you had before have disappeared. You have collapsed the negative anchor.

Fixing your phobias

Phobias are exaggerated anchored responses to everyday situations – they can cause muscle tension, hyperventilation, perspiration and dizziness. When a phobic response is being experienced, your internal dialogue and imagery will be predicting dire consequences. Phobias are irrational fears – as opposed to the rational fears caused by things that actually happen, such as the house being on fire. Because phobias are irrational, they are relatively easy to overcome. NLP is very effective in fixing all kinds of phobias, including fear of bridges, confined spaces, open spaces, flying, lifts, spiders, bees, birds, frogs and snakes. This even extends to phobias about wet hair in the shower plughole, oranges and bananas!

> NLP is very effective in fixing all kinds of phobias

In our experience, many people try to hide their phobias and avoid situations where they may have to face their fear. This is because they perceive their problem as being ridiculous and try to avoid the embarrassment caused by their reaction. At a deep level, this can have an adverse effect on self-esteem, as a phobia is often thought of as a weakness. Underlying any phobia is a belief about what will happen in the situation causing the phobia. For example, when Paul was a teenager, he choked on an orange. Over time, he unconsciously anchored a negative response to this experience. Eventually, this became a phobic reaction to oranges, to such an extent that he had to leave the room whenever someone began to peel an orange. He believed that if he ate an orange he would choke.

The test for whether a person has a phobia or not – as opposed to being merely very concerned – is that they will react very physically to even the *thought* of their fear. Because it is the thought that produces the reaction, it can be eliminated without having to relive the experience.

If a phobia is affecting your enjoyment of life and/or your self-esteem, use the following technique – it has a very high success rate. We suggest that you familiarise yourself with the procedure before using it. This will enable you to complete the exercise without the distraction of referring to the notes.

---

brilliant example

During one of our programmes, Colin, a delegate moved the curtains to shade us from the sun. As he did so, a large spider ran out and he literally flew across the room to the door. Another delegate removed the spider and Colin returned to his seat highly embarrassed. He explained the strength of his phobia and we suggested that, if he would like to deal with it, we could do so very quickly.

After a ten-minute phobia fix, Colin asked if he could go and find a spider. We found one in the conservatory and he was quite happy to stand and look at it from a distance of 6cm (2½ inches).

Fast phobia fix

We are going to ask you to do a few things very quickly in your mind so that your phobia will never bother you again.

1 Imagine that you are sitting in a cinema and, on the screen, there is a black and white still picture in which you see yourself just before your last experience of having the phobic response.

2 Now imagine that you are floating out of your body and up to the projection room, where you can see yourself sitting in the cinema. You can also see yourself in the still picture on the screen.

3 Turn the snapshot on the screen into a black and white movie and watch it until just after the unpleasant phobic experience. When you get to the end, stop it as a still. Now jump inside the picture and run it backwards in colour. Everything in the film will happen in reverse – people walking backwards, talking backwards and the scenery moving backwards.

4 This completes the exercise. Take a few deep breaths and test the results by thinking about what it was that you used to be phobic about.

Reframing

The exercises in this chapter will have helped you to work with the emotions attached to your thinking and given you access to your inner resources. There may be times when the *way* you are thinking is creating a barrier. You can change your perspective completely by reframing this kind of thinking in a number of ways. In the same way that placing a new frame around a picture can give it a whole new appearance, placing a new frame around your thoughts can give you a very different perspective.

▶ **brilliant** example

Frank was 'at his wits' end' (his words) trying to get his youngest son Timmy to keep the house tidy. The relationship became increasingly strained as Frank continued to lay down the law. He often raised his voice and Timmy responded by retreating into silence and making himself scarce. The situation became progressively worse and Timmy's performance at school suffered. Frank explained that he was lost for a way to help Timmy 'get his act together'. Timmy was getting a hard time from his dad and his falling marks at school were a direct result of stress.

We offered Frank the following reframe.

It appears that you have been pushing Timmy to meet a certain standard of tidiness, which is causing him a good deal of stress and creating distance between you. His untidiness may, in fact, be a phase that kids of his age go through and a sign that he's behaving normally. By letting him be a normal teenager, he might not be so stressed and be able to focus better on his schoolwork.

In short, Frank was offered a reframe that moved him from thinking 'my boy is untidy' to 'my boy is untidy, which is normal behaviour for any teenager'. It helped Frank to realise that his behaviour towards Timmy had caused the breakdown in the relationship between them. He immediately stopped hounding him about being untidy and started to help him more with his schoolwork.

This type of reframe changes the meaning of the situation. Another type of reframe shifts the meaning between contexts. For example, a person who may be highly critical of other peoples' ideas might be perceived by his team as being difficult or negative. However, the presence of a critic on the team can be very useful when evaluating ideas resulting from a creative brainstorm. It's not that the behaviour of the critic is a problem, it's more a case of knowing how best to use that particular skill. This type of reframe puts the behaviour into a positive frame in another context.

A common cause of frustration in couples is demonstrated in the next example.

brilliant example

Fiona likes to be on time and is obsessive about dates, times, schedules and lists. Mike, Fiona's partner, is the exact opposite, preferring to take a more relaxed and laid-back approach to life. Mike was feeling torn by wanting to please Fiona while at the same time being unable to rationalise the pressure she was putting him under.

After some coaching, Mike realised that Fiona's ability as an organiser was useful in many ways, including remembering family birthdays, shopping, planning holidays and generally running the family very effectively. Having reframed his thinking in this way, the pressure eased. It was attached to the way he had been thinking, not to the circumstances.

Don't think that, think this!

Any reframe is simply saying 'don't think of it that way, think of it this way'. It's not that, it's this! You can apply simple reframes to all kinds of situations that are not working out as you would like.

A problem can only exist in your mind – outside your mind there are only sets of circumstances. That you call a circumstance a problem is

> one person's problem is another's source of motivation

indicative of your way of thinking. One person's problem is another's source of motivation. So, it really matters how you think about any situation you find yourself in because it has consequences.

The words **this** and **that** are used many times during the course of a day, but, when used with tasks and people – for example 'that task' or 'this person' – they indicate whether the speaker is associated with or dissociated from what they are referring to. Where there is a positive intention towards a task/person, there is likely to be a positive mindset around it – it's a **this**. When there is no positive intention towards it, there is likely to be a negative mindset around it – it's a **that**. Being dissociated from something is a source of procrastination. If you could choose not to get involved, then there would be no issue, but, when you *have* to get involved because it's your job to do so, then you are forced to associate, which is when negative feelings can take hold of your thinking. In situations of forced association, it is useful to reframe your thinking and turn **that** into **this** with a positive intention.

There are four key principles involved.

1   You can be either *associated* **(this)** or *dissociated* **(that)** with tasks and people. When you are associated in a positive way, you are emotionally connected and likely to achieve better results than when you have put distance between yourself and the task or person, thus becoming dissociated. Poor performance results from 'forced association' with a **that** – when you perform a **that** task without a clear positive intention, you are forcing yourself to associate with it and so the emotional connection is likely to be negative. This is a recipe for poor performance.

2   Having a conscious positive intention prepares the way for success – all your intentions are positive for you, even though it may not appear that way to other people. Your unconscious mind may be telling you not to go ahead with an unpleasant task because its positive intention is to keep you feeling good. Having a clear positive intention and looking for the good in the task allows you to take control of your success. Having no positive intention prepares the

way for struggle. Just as a clear positive intention clears the way for success, so not having one causes you to struggle. Your unconscious intention will be to feel better and look for ways that mean you don't have to undertake an unpleasant task or meet someone who makes you feel uncomfortable. In doing so, you cause yourself stress and discomfort.

3   When you exaggerate the absurdity of the way you are thinking about a situation, you prepare the ground for change. You can find absurdity in almost anything and use it to create change. An example demonstrating this follows in the next section.

4   Changing **that** to **this** is primarily a matter of focusing on what is good and having a positive intention. The concept of yin and yang demonstrates that, to achieve balance and flow in life, everything must contain an element of its opposite. Hot will contain elements of cold, good will contain elements of bad and vice versa. So, every **that** must contain an element of **this**. Unfortunately, while you are focusing on **that** you are oblivious to the **this**, which is undoubtedly present. Your results will be more successful if you choose to stay focused on **this** and allow it to develop and grow.

There can be any number of reasons behind you considering something or someone as a **that**. For example, they can be:

● activities you don't enjoy and don't look forward to
● work that you don't feel fully competent to complete to a satisfactory standard
● someone or something you have negative beliefs about
● activities that conflict with a personal value
● someone you find difficult or frustrating to be with.

Using absurdity to create a change in thinking

You can find absurdity in just about anything. Consider the statement, 'I have to have dinner on the table by 6pm every day'. This implies that all the family members will be hungry and ready to eat at exactly the same time every day. The likelihood of that being the case is remote and, therefore, the statement is absurd.

This technique takes the absurdity in your thinking and exaggerates it. In doing so, your situation becomes so ridiculous that you will want to change your view and reframe it because it is too painful to continue thinking in the old way.

---

brilliant example

Peter was a project manager who was a real stickler for detail and procedure. He had been given responsibility for a major project involving Simon. Simon became more and more anxious whenever he thought about the project.

Peter and Simon had clashed from the outset. Simon didn't know how to deal with Peter when he insisted on introducing details that Simon believed were unnecessary at the meetings. This began to affect his ability to contribute rationally. He would sneer and make derogatory comments about Peter's style of management in front of the project team. When questioned about the situation, Simon replied, 'He needs to learn a lesson if he's going to get on – I'll teach him, don't you worry'.

Simon was offered the following reframe.

So Simon, it seems you want to go on feeling bad about this relationship, don't you? You are going to continue to snipe at Peter and have everyone else laugh and snigger at you behind your back. You don't even mind that they perceive you to be behaving like a child. The project will suffer and your emotional energy will be tied up in creating negative feelings towards Peter, so you will have very little left for creativity around the project.

However, you won't mind that because teaching Peter a lesson is so much more important to you than building good relationships and getting the project completed successfully. Your antagonistic behaviour will serve you well when you find yourself not being invited on to the team for future projects. You may even find yourself without a role at all and that's OK because the most important thing here is to make Peter look silly, isn't it?'

This technique may appear a little harsh, but, with the right person, it could be the most effective tool to use. In this case, Simon is the type to allow his ego to get in the way, so the technique had to be stronger than his overinflated ego. What Simon received was a reframe that moved him from thinking 'Peter needs to be taught a lesson' to 'my career is more important than the way I feel about Peter'. This caused sufficient pain to Simon's ego for him to let go of the need to teach Peter a lesson and make positive adjustments to his thinking and behaviour.

Focus on a positive intention

The absurdity technique may do the trick for some people (we hope you tried it out on your own situation with state X) and sometimes you may need a little more positive encouragement. However negatively you view a situation or a person, there is always some good to be found.

brilliant example

Michelle was having a problem with her flatmate, who seemed to be interfering in her life. She took it to mean that her flatmate didn't trust her to make her own decisions about boyfriends. Michelle began to mistrust her own judgement and became withdrawn, refusing invitations to nights out.

When questioned, she said that her flatmate didn't want her to have a good time and was jealous of her boyfriends. This frame of thinking caused a deep rift in the friendship.

Michelle was offered the following reframe.

Michelle, could it be that your flatmate cares about you and doesn't want to see you get hurt? Maybe she has had a painful relationship and doesn't want you to experience the same pain. Perhaps focusing on the perceived jealousy is keeping you from noticing ways in which she really does care. However it may seem to you, the reality could be very different. If she did care for you, what is it that she does that will tell you this?

Michelle decided to look for evidence that her flatmate really did care about her well-being. She discovered lots of small things she did for her that had previously gone unnoticed. The relationship improved and they healed the rift. The point at which this situation turned around was when Michelle flipped her **that** mindset to **this** mindset and created a positive intention to find the good in her flatmate.

Flipping a **that** to a **this**

1   Think of a task you really don't enjoy doing that causes you to procrastinate or one you do very quickly to get it out of the way. Whichever you choose, it causes you bad feelings and, possibly, leads you to perform it below your usual standard.

2   Create a conscious positive intention relating to completing the task and begin to focus on the intention.

3   Either use the absurdity technique described above or begin to develop the positive aspects of the task or both. How absurd is it that you have been thinking of the task in that way? Keep looking for the good and release your mind from the negative aspects of the task.

Thinking in **this** way will allow your mind to be creative and come up with solutions and ideas rather than becoming stressed by the bad feelings associated with **that**-type thinking.

> thinking in **this** way will allow your mind to be creative and come up with solutions and ideas

brilliant tip

Every new skill you attempt requires a degree of practice. The more you practise these techniques, the more you will reprogramme your thinking to create new feelings and behaviour that serve you well. Take one technique at a time and practise it several times on issues that are real for you before moving on to the next technique.

CHAPTER 4

Organise your thinking for successful results

So far we have focused on how one thought leads to another and how your thinking determines your behaviour. It's your behaviour that has an impact on the people around you and that people respond to. Your attitude of mind is an important factor in forming your behaviour. So, if you have an aggressive attitude, your behaviour will take on aggressive qualities; if you have an attitude of superiority, your body language will send that message to others; a relaxed attitude will result in a relaxed posture.

From this we can see that your attitude directly affects your behaviour and consists of a collection of experiences generalised into a set of values and a complex web of beliefs. In *Changing Belief Systems with NLP* (Meta Publications, 1990), Robert Dilts developed a universal model to explain how this works. You can use it to organise your thinking for successful results in any context. You consider each of five levels of thinking in relation to any specific purpose:

your attitude directly affects your behaviour

1 identity
2 values and beliefs
3 capability
4 behaviour
5 environment.

Awareness of these levels will make it easy to choose the most effective NLP technique for the change you wish to make. The key to using this model is to begin with a clearly defined purpose.

Is your purpose crystal clear?

In all situations, you have an intention. Often this is unconscious – you engage with other people or undertake tasks without first thinking what you intend to achieve. For example, what is your intention when having a particular conversation with your partner? Is it to inform, gain support, satisfy your need to be heard, seek attention or something else? What is your intention when undertaking a part-time job or choosing a new career? Is it to leave behind a tedious or stressful job, do something you have aspired to for some time, increase your income or have flexible working hours?

If your intention is unclear, then you run the risk of behaving in a way that will sabotage your best efforts and leave you feeling dissatisfied. A classic example of this is when someone is feeling bad about his or her life in some way and decides to move to a different city or country for a fresh start. At a deep level, the intention is to remove the bad feelings, which have grown over time. What often happens is that the new life follows exactly the same pattern of events as the previous one.

Having a clear sense of purpose will enable you to make a conscious choice about how you approach situations. It will bring your deepest intentions to the surface and determine the role you play in the pursuit of your purpose. Having clarified your purpose, the next step is to organise your thinking within each of the five levels of alignment listed above.

1 What role are you playing?

In life, you play many different work, family and societal roles. You may split your time between being a parent, sibling, provider, chairperson, technician, leader, carer or any number of combinations of roles. What's important here is not the *label* for your role, but how you define it. This has an impact on your results. The manager who defines her role as taskmaster and organiser will elicit a very different response from her team than the manager who defines her role as people developer. Children of parents who define their role as protectors will grow up very differently from children whose parents define their role as nurturers. The teacher with a role of disciplinarian and controller will elicit very different results from another who defines her role as challenger and learning facilitator.

The role you define in the pursuit of your purpose will interact with your values and beliefs, which determine what you pay attention to and what you ignore.

2 What values and beliefs do you hold?

If you are a nurturing parent, you will probably have strong values relating to providing opportunities for life experiences for your children. A manager who believes in getting the best out of people will have strong values concerning trust and the potential of the team. A teacher creating a positive learning environment will value discovery, exploration and creativity.

These values will be supported by any number of beliefs. The nature of a belief causes you to focus on your values and proves the belief to be true. So, whatever you believe to be true, you will seek evidence to prove it and ignore evidence to the contrary. This is why it is so important to make sure your beliefs are empowering you to achieve the results you desire. For example, a teacher with the

> it is important to make sure your beliefs are empowering you

belief that a child has a learning difficulty will continue to reinforce the difficulty. On the other hand, a teacher with the belief that the child has potential, and the challenge is to find a way to release it, will undoubtedly achieve better results.

3 Are you limiting your true capability?

Your values and beliefs have a direct impact on your capability. Quite simply, if you believe that you can, then you will find a way of doing so. If you believe that you can't, then you won't bother to look for a way. Empowering beliefs unlock capability and limiting beliefs act as a barrier.

Limiting beliefs stop you from putting effort into things. It's like the kaleidoscope is stuck in the same pattern – you have the power to change it but refrain from doing so because you are either unaware or unsure of the consequences. Eventually the pattern becomes dull and loses its excitement. Once you believe that it's not possible to change it, then you will find every excuse to make this true. It is very common for people to use illness as an excuse for continuing to believe that they can't achieve something. You only have to look around to find many examples of people who have achieved great things, against the odds, due to the power of their belief.

if you value something enough you will generate a belief that it is possible to achieve

Values and beliefs work together – if you value something enough you will generate a belief that it is possible to achieve and put your energy into finding a way.

brilliant example

Sally opted out of a language exercise, saying that she was no good at English. She explained how her English teacher had encouraged her to pursue a career with numbers because her English was so poor. She followed this advice, took a job as a junior accountant and disliked it intensely. She left after three years to work as a shop assistant, from where her career developed.

On being quizzed about her current role, she revealed that she had been promoted to the customer services team and now writes letters for the department – and really enjoys it. Sally also receives regular praise for the quality and creative nature of her letters. However, despite this praise, she still maintained the belief that she was no good at English and developed the habit of withdrawing from any activities based on language. The acceptance of her teacher's belief limited Sally's natural ability in this area for many years.

4 Is your behaviour aligned with your thinking?

Your behaviour is a result of the way you have organised your thinking at each of the three levels above. Once Sally was able to change her belief about her capability in English, it opened up a whole new range of activities for her. She began writing short stories and articles and even attempted some poetry.

Some of your behaviour will be working well for you, other aspects will not. Once behaviour becomes a habit, it is almost unrecognisable by you – until someone points it out.

brilliant example

A group of elderly couples were walking arm in arm through a hotel lobby to dinner. One lady was limping and carefully holding on to a man's arm. As she limped across the room, she suddenly realised that she had left her glass of wine at the bar and took off with a determined stride to retrieve it. She had forgotten to limp. The limp was not in her leg but in her mind.

Which parts of your behaviour are no longer of use to you? What tugs are you feeling? What would happen if you gave your kaleidoscope a small twist?

5 Are you having an impact on your environment?

The way you organise your thinking at the four levels above will determine the impact you have on your physical environment. Limiting beliefs and an unclear purpose create stress. The blame for stress is often placed on external factors in the environment. This moves the focus away from self and, in doing so, takes away the power of influence. With empowering beliefs and a strong sense of purpose, you are likely to take responsibility for changing your environment. Even unconsciously, you are likely to have a positive impact. Often you may believe that the environment is causing you some stress and feel emotionally tugged. The stronger the limiting beliefs about your capability, the more likely it is that you will recognise what is wrong in the world yet do nothing positive to create change. People who change things believe that they can.

> people who change things believe that they can

The first step towards taking control is identifying the level at which a tug is taking place.

▶ brilliant example

Jamie is of Middle Eastern origin and settled in this country with his beautiful wife Anika. He was finding life hard in the UK – not getting along with his colleagues at work, his social circle was getting smaller and he felt increasingly isolated. He blamed the culture in the UK and felt unable to fit in. He decided that it was time to move back to his home country.

Anika explained to us that Jamie was exactly the same in his home country. She didn't want to move back and knew that his problem was nothing to do with country or culture. Jamie was merely shifting the responsibility for how he was feeling on to the culture and country. Anika knew that the real problem was Jamie's shyness.

Fortunately, it took only one coaching session with Jamie for him to become aware of his shyness pattern and learn some strategies for making friends and being a more confident person.

Are you aligned with your purpose?

Sometimes a change in behaviour does not follow a change in thinking. Have you ever been in a position where you have done something you didn't want to do? Perhaps you did it to please someone and then felt you had done yourself a disservice. Maybe you made a decision to lead a healthier lifestyle and take up running or yoga, but, when the time came to attend a class or go to the gym, you let yourself down and reverted to your regular unhealthy habit. It's at times like these that you feel the instinctive tug of misalignment.

> Have you ever done something you didn't want to do?

In NLP, this state of misalignment resulting in a behaviour that doesn't fit with the other levels is called 'incongruence'. Deep inside you want to act a certain way, but, when the time comes, you resist the inner urge and maybe tell yourself 'not this time, maybe next time'. That is incongruence and it is not something success thrives on.

Success requires congruence, which means an alignment of all the levels, from purpose all the way through to behaviour. Only then can you affect your environment in the way that you really want. Creating such an alignment is the process of building self-confidence as you then know that you have executed a change of mind and acted accordingly. Being able to recognise when you are being incongruent is the first step towards making your desired change happen.

The feeling of incongruence doesn't have to stem from a major life realisation – it can happen during the course of a business meeting or in a conversation with a partner. So, whatever you are doing, it pays to be able to recognise feelings of incongruence.

When you take a close look at the times when you are successful, chances are you also feel happy and confident. Sure, you can imagine all kinds of bad things happening if you choose to, but, when you are engaged in the act of doing something superbly well, you will be at your happiest. There is a saying, 'if you have to ask yourself if you are happy then you are probably not'. Happiness is a state of mind and you arrive at it by being congruent in your actions.

Happy people attract happy people

In the same way that similar thoughts congregate in clusters, so do people. If you feel depressed, you will attract depressed people and upbeat people will avoid you. If you gain the skills to help people to improve their lives, those who need you will find you. If you decide to be unhappy, you will be. That's how life works – it will bring you what you express with your whole being. Cynical people keep each other company and strengthen their cynical attitude. The key message here is, what energy are you giving off and who and what are you attracting?

Your feelings of incongruence are likely to transmit signals that other people will perceive as confusing and unpredictable. As a consequence, they may judge you as being unreliable.

You hear people referring to others as being smug, with a chip on their shoulder, arrogant, brash, stand-offish, stuck up, cold fish. These are all interpretations of the way a person is communicating. It may be true, but, as soon as you have interpreted a person's behaviour, you have also chosen to relate to them with that judgement in your mind. The real truth lies beneath the behaviour in the kaleidoscope of their thinking. What is being picked up is a misalignment between levels – the result of the unconscious tugs referred to earlier. The key is to develop 'curiosity' about what is causing a person to behave in such a way, rather than interpret the behaviour you see. Then, you reduce your chances of falling into the trap of acting according to a misinterpretation and increase the likelihood that you will begin to understand the person and communicate effectively.

In our work, we meet all kinds of people. They come to us because they feel stuck with some aspect of their life. We have worked with managers who are not making the progress they want with their team, life coaches who are struggling to make ends meet, couples who have lost the excitement in their lives, directors who are petrified at the thought of giving a presentation to the board, professionals who are snowed under with tasks, stressed and losing sleep, workers who are not meeting their employer's expectations of performance, people with obsessions, phobias, stress, anger, frustration, apathy and all kinds of behaviour patterns that are causing problems. We meet people from all walks of life who are limiting their potential to succeed and be brilliant in all kinds of situations. The one thing they have in common is a feeling of incongruence when they think about the conflict they are living with. What they discover is how one frustration or problem is related to others, such as weight loss or gain, smoking, cluttered thinking, frequent illness, low self-esteem, being able to feel and patterns of broken relationships.

When you feel under stress due to personal difficulties, your mind has a wonderful capacity to put your problems behind a veil. This allows you to have some stability and maintain the status quo of your life. However, passion and energy also become masked behind the veil. Even though you can create a smokescreen for your thinking, your body is not easily deceived.

> even though you can create a smokescreen for your thinking, your body is not easily deceived

You can fool your mind but not your body

Your mind and body are part of the same energy system and interact with each other in response to external stimuli. When you are having a tough day and your mind is working flat out to meet deadlines, stress accumulates in your body – for example, you may become tense and your breathing erratic. Your body will react to whatever changes your mind goes through and vice versa.

> your body gives signals to other people, that something is incongruent

Your body gives signals to other people, so, even though you may be able to create a smokescreen and veil your problems in your own mind, others will intuitively know that something is incongruent. The only way to deal with this is to remove the veil of your thinking and create a change.

One of the people Bandler and Grinder modelled in the early days of creating NLP was Virginia Satir, a highly effective family therapist. Virginia achieved very quick results by using a unique way to help individual family members become aware of their incongruent behaviour. The behaviour she identified in *Peoplemaking* (Science and Behaviour Books, 1972) is not exclusive to dysfunctional families. You only need to look around to see examples everywhere.

Satir categories

Virginia devised four categories of behaviour that she identified as being responsible for many family conflicts, and one that can be used to resolve conflict and bring people together.

Distracter

Distracters seek attention to compensate for their feelings of loneliness or inadequacy. The positive intention behind their behaviour is to protect them from facing up to things. Distracting behaviour includes removing a hair from your jacket lapel while you are talking, sabotaging a conversation by making a joke, interrupting a conversation, frequently changing the subject. There are many other types of distracting behaviour that people use to deflect attention from a subject that may be reminding them of their feelings of loneliness and inadequacy.

Distracter patterns are usually learned early in life when you are at your most vulnerable to what is happening around you. At the time, the pattern is like a coping strategy, but it can become a long-term habit. Luckily we know how to break habits.

▶ brilliant example

Derek was a forthright person with lots of confidence and intelligence. He was a senior director with a retail company and was getting squeezed out by other directors because they said that he was 'far too arrogant'. He had developed a habit of kicking or throwing around any small items within his reach. It was as if he were releasing some negative energy as a response whenever he felt he wasn't being listened to or acknowledged, as if to say 'Hey, I'm here, can you watch me now.'

Derek was astounded at the number of years he had been holding on to this pattern and, after coaching, realised that it was no longer required. He was then able to relax and respond in a more mature way without needing to be the centre of attention.

Placater

The placater is out to please – talking in an ingratiating way, never disagreeing and always seeking approval. Feelings of an inability to cope alone create a martyr or 'yes man' (or woman!) A placater is often the first person to accept the blame when things go wrong.

▶ brilliant example

Jenny just couldn't stop herself from saying 'Sorry' at the beginning of almost everything she said. It was such a habit, that it just popped out all the time – 'Sorry for asking, but ...' or 'Sorry, did you want to use this?' or 'Sorry, sorry, sorry, I didn't think to ask, I hope you're not upset, I'm ever so sorry.' Jenny would say sorry for entering a room, sorry for being in the way, and sorry for watching the wrong channel on TV.

Blamer

Blamers find fault, never accepting responsibility themselves, but, rather, always blaming someone or something else. They feel unsuccessful and lonely. They often suffer from high blood pressure and come across as aggressive and tyrannical. They will tell you what is wrong with things and whose fault it is and, in doing so, become powerless to do anything about it. By blaming external factors, they have absolved themselves of responsibility.

▶ brilliant example

Damian had a set way of doing things. He appeared outspoken and stubborn to those who knew him. The combination of *away from* and *procedural* metaprogrammes caused him to 'know' the right way to do things and he would blame those who disagreed when things didn't go his way.

Computer

Computer-like behaviour is that which is very correct and proper, but displays no feeling. The voice is dry and monotone and the body often very still and precise in its movements, which are minimal, masking a feeling of vulnerability.

example

Jo had worked with computers for a long time. Her main means of communication was via e-mail and she became awkward when in the company of others. Consequently, she remained as still as possible, speaking only when spoken to and her movements were controlled and deliberate.

Leveller

This is the category to be in! Levellers have few threats to their self-esteem. Words, voice tone, body movements and facial expressions all give the same message. Levellers apologise for an action, not for existing. They have no need to blame, be sub-servient, retreat into computer behaviour or to be constantly on the move. They are great communicators and have the ability to build bridges in relationships, heal impasses and build self-esteem.

The leveller's response is a real-time, congruent response. All the other responses are the result of negative internal feelings causing words and actions to be incongruent. It is very easy, under pressure, to respond to a situation with 'It's not my fault' or 'I'm sorry, it's my fault again' or laugh inappropriately or show no emotion at all. These behaviours don't allow you to seek out rational solutions. The leveller's response is the most effective behaviour for solving problems creatively.

Levellers:

● look for solutions

● have a conscious, positive intention behind everything they do

● hold strong positive beliefs about themselves and others

● operate from strong personal values

- store positive mind images
- are flexible in their behaviour when communicating with others
- establish rapport before trying to influence.

---

brilliant example

Kieran was the Chief Executive of a pharmaceutical company. His team had a high respect for him due to his ability to level with them. He was able to drive the business, admit when he made a mistake, recognise ideas and ability in others and have fun while keeping a cool head.

All these attributes can be learnt via NLP using the techniques in this book.

brilliant tip

Be careful what you think – it can so easily become a self-fulfilling prophecy.

CHAPTER 5

Using rapport to build successful relationships

We all need people in our lives – to love us and to be loved, to buy from and sell to, to coach and be coached, to teach and learn from and enjoy life with. The results of your interactions with each individual you meet will be determined by your ability to get on with them, be influenced by them and influence their thinking and behaviour. Whatever you do, your ability to influence others in all kinds of ways is important if you want to be more than a passive onlooker. Whether you are parenting, buying, selling, managing, leading, coaching, mentoring, relaxing or having fun, your degree of success in all these areas will come down to your ability to influence, and this requires skill in building rapport quickly.

> your ability to influence others is important if you want to be more than a passive onlooker

Think about times when other people have tried to influence you. Perhaps you have experienced a pushy sales assistant or a prescriptive boss or an overbearing partner. How did you feel at the time? Think of a time when you were enticed by a sales assistant – what did he or she do that enticed you? Would you warm to someone whom you felt had no respect for you? Would you feel comfortable with a person who made no attempt to understand your needs? Probably not. Strong rapport is required to hold up a strong relationship – much like strong foundations will hold up a tall building.

Developing your ability to build rapport can help build confidence and contribute towards a more rewarding lifestyle with friends, colleagues and family. Rapport often develops naturally and you probably don't notice when it's happening. We expect you already have rapport with many people, but there will be occasions when a person who is important to your success is not on your wavelength and you will need to work at building a relationship with that person.

The role of respect in building rapport

In order to build rapport, you must first decide to respect the other person's perspective. How can you build rapport with someone if the outcome is uncertain or you don't feel confident in your role in that situation or you have a conflict of values? If you attempt to fake rapport, you will get caught out. People pick up your true motives and feelings from your body language and tone of voice, so, if you are insincere, it will show.

If you want to create rapport with someone, you must do it from a position of respect and a genuine need to understand them and seek win–win outcomes. When you feel congruent with your outcomes, identity, values and beliefs, then your behaviour will follow naturally.

Using what you do naturally – matching and mirroring

Have you ever watched two people deep in conversation? If they are both fully engaged in the exchange, they will unconsciously copy each other's body postures, movements, voice tone, pace and breathing. Sometimes they do it exactly – matching – and other times they are mirror images of each other – mirroring. It's like dancing to a rhythm.

You can use this knowledge and do it deliberately to provide the foundation for building rapport with anyone you choose. In NLP, it is called matching and mirroring.

Essentially, it works like this. People like people who are like them, so a sure way of building rapport with others is to be like them. You can build relation-

> people like people who are like them, so be like them

ships and influence a wider variety of people by becoming consciously aware of what you do when you naturally have rapport. Equally, when rapport has been lost, you can take decisive action to rebuild it.

Using your body to build rapport

There is a common misconception about body language – you can interpret what it means. If you base your approach to people on your interpretation of their body language, you will get it wrong much of the time. Interpretation will not get you very far.

It is more useful to use what you notice about a person's body language in the matching and mirroring process. So, crossed arms doesn't necess- arily mean that somebody is closed – they could just be

> there is a common misconception about body language – you can interpret what it means

feeling comfortable that way. If you also fold your arms, you will be joining them in their 'dance' and they will feel comfortable with you. However, knowing how people have a tendency to interpret body language and often get it wrong, you need to be aware of your own as others are likely to be making judgements about you from your posture, gestures and tone of voice, too.

Matching and mirroring body language is a highly effective method of creating rapport. At first it may seem a little wooden, but, as you practise it and learn to do it naturally, no one notices.

It becomes an unconscious process. To be proficient at it requires you to overcome any apprehensions you may have. It's like learning anything – practising it makes it easier to do. Things that you can usefully match include:

- physiology – body posture, position, movement, gestures (when you are talking), breathing
- voice – tone, speed, volume, pitch, timbre, rhythm
- language – key words
- values – (personal and intrinsic) what people hold as being true and important
- experience – common interests.

Matching and mirroring take place at the behavioural level. Think back to a time when you felt awkward building rapport and it just wasn't working, no matter what you tried. What was going on for you? Was it anything to do with the mirroring and matching or was it more to do with what was going on inside your head? Using the above list to match and mirror, how would you create rapport with a two-year-old child? How about a teenager? A pensioner? A particular person you want to influence at work?

How to match and mirror to create rapport

1 Think of someone you have not seen eye-to-eye with, where a better relationship would be good for you both. Imagine meeting that person.

2 Notice his or her posture and body language, then match or mirror it. You don't need total precision when matching. Are the arms folded? Is the breathing fast, slow, shallow or deep? Are the legs crossed? Notice the gestures used and use the same gestures when you are speaking. Raise or lower your voice tone and pace to match. Above all, be curious about what he or she has to say, and acknowledge that you are listening. When you

speak, use the same words as he or she does wherever possible rather than substituting your own preferred words – don't use 'shop' for their 'store'. This may seem unnatural, but it works. It is giving the other person a very strong message that you are a lot like him or her.

Time taken creating and building rapport will pay dividends in the influencing process. Be open and willing to be influenced by the other person's perspectives. If you attempt to gain rapport and yet show no interest in understanding the other person, you are unlikely to succeed. Lasting rapport requires sincerity and recep-

> lasting rapport requires sincerity and receptivity

tivity – you need to really understand the other person's unique perspectives on how things are and not push yours on to them.

brilliant example

Laura was struggling to understand her manager. Whenever she designed a complicated conference, she would present it to him and he would invariably ask about a small detail, such as what times the coffee breaks were. She felt that he was devaluing all the hard work she had put in until we explained how his need for detail was driving his behaviour – it had nothing to do with Laura.

Next time Laura was in that situation, she simply pointed out the times of the coffee breaks and he was perfectly happy and didn't feel the need to check anything further. As a result, his trust in Laura's ability to attend to detail grew and so did the autonomy he gave her.

Pacing and leading

Having created rapport, you now have a foundation for influencing. Generally speaking, a person is unlikely to accept your views, opinions and goals unless they can form some attachment to them. Just telling a person what you want is not a smart option. First, make sure that you have strong rapport, then gently lead the person towards your thinking and create as much attachment for them as you can.

Pacing is the ongoing process of matching the other person's unique perception, thus strengthening rapport. The same applies in group meetings and presentations where you might begin by pacing common views or experiences. Once you have gained a good level of rapport by pacing, begin to lead and influence the other person or group. Check if the other person is willing to follow you by changing your physiology and noticing what happens. If you have rapport they will follow you. If rapport is lost during leading, revert to pacing and regain rapport before continuing to lead to a desired outcome. The general view in NLP is that you need twice as much pacing as leading.

Taking the lead with your ideas

When you introduce a new topic to a conversation, unless the topic is popular you risk breaking rapport. Why should anyone want to listen to what you have to say? Most people attempt to introduce their ideas into a conversation and justify them as we all like to defend and protect what we consider to be important. A smarter way of getting your ideas accepted is to connect them with the ideas already held by the other person. You are then able to make a smooth transition to your topic. Minds like to be led to new ideas.

> minds like to be led to new ideas

People communicate using differently sized chunks of information along a continuum – detail and global being at each extreme. You can use this concept to pace and lead elegantly.

Here's a simple example of how information comes in chunks. Take the word 'tree'. A tree is part of a wood, which is vegetation, which is part of the ecosystem. So, here, we have 'chunked up' from tree to ecosystem. You can just as easily 'chunk down' from tree to oak to branch, to leaves. You can also move in a lateral direction from any level. For example, a lateral move from the word 'oak' would give us types of tree, such as birch, fir, pine, coconut and so on. There are only three directions you can take during a conversation – up, down and lateral.

Here's how you might use chunking to gain financial support for a project.

You arrive at your manager's desk to find him deep in conversation about the latest cricket test match. You are not going to be very popular and probably won't get a result if you begin talking about money immediately. You need to find a way to lead him from 'test match' to 'financial support'.

In this example, there are seven levels, but, in reality, a conversation can range over any number of levels.

1	Corporate finance	
2	Sponsorship	**Finance**
3	Professional sport	
4	**Test match**	International football, golf, tennis, rugby
5	Teams and clubs	Australia, England, West Indies, Pakistan
6	Players	Umpires, spectators, organisers
7	Batsman	Bowler, fielder, wicketkeeper

From 'test match', you may choose to chunk up to professional sport, sponsorship and corporate finance or down to specific teams, the players and the roles they play. Here is how the conversation might go – notice how Kate joins the conversation at level 4 and takes it to level 2, from where she can naturally introduce her idea for sponsorship.

Peter (manager): Did you see any of the test cricket yesterday, Joe? (level 4)

Joe: Yes, isn't X playing well? (level 6)

Peter: I love test cricket. I find it relaxing and exciting at the same time. (level 4)

Kate (arriving): I saw the match yesterday, too. My partner is a cricket addict (level 4). In fact, he is a sports fanatic full stop. (level 4)

Peter: Oh really? What other sports does he like? (level 4)

Kate: He is a member of the Y football club (level 5) and gets to see quite a few matches from the sponsor's lounge because he works for the Z software company. (level 5) They did really well last year out of a new product they introduced and sponsor Y is giving them loads of publicity. (level 2) They can't seem to do anything wrong at the moment.

Peter: Perhaps we should think about sponsoring a club? (level 1)

Kate: Perhaps when we have got this new marketing campaign off the ground it will give us the publicity we need to be able to approach a club. (level 1) I've actually got the figures here for you to look at Peter. (level 2)

By working the levels in this way, you will be able to chunk to a level where you can cross over to your topic. In this case, the crossover was reached at level 2 when Peter mentioned sponsorship as it was then a simple step to the topic of finance. What you are doing in a strategy like this is joining in with the other person's value and staying with it, then linking that value in a subtle way with your topic. It's about facilitating a smooth transition from topic to topic.

Here are some more examples.

● Getting your young son from 'PlayStation' to 'room tidying'.

You: What level are you on with your new game?

Son: Level 6.

You: What do you have to do to get to level 7?

Son: Shoot all the aliens in the way.

You: Wow, that'll tidy up all those aliens won't it? How many aliens are there in your bedroom?

Son: Don't know.

You: Shall we count them?

Son: OK.

You: Now, what shall we do with them to clear them out of the way?

● Getting your partner from 'football' to 'holidays'.

You: What's the score?

Partner: 2–1 to United.

You: It looks really sunny where they are playing. Is it in this country?

Partner: No, it's in Barcelona.

You: Wouldn't you rather be there watching the match in all that glorious sunshine?

Partner: Of course I would.

You: Why don't we book a holiday in Spain and soak up some of that lovely sun?

● Getting your hypochondriac parent from 'what's wrong with me' to 'let's go out somewhere'.

Parent: I feel really ill today. I really don't know what's wrong with me.

You: Really? What's been happening?

Parent: I keep getting dizzy spells when I get up out of my chair.

You: Dizzy spells? What are they like?

Parent: It's like having little stars in front of my eyes. They soon go away but it frightens me when it's happening.

You: Stars are really pretty. Why don't you try and capture them for a moment before they disappear? In fact, today I am going to take you to see lots of stars, including the biggest of them all – your granddaughter. We are going to the children's pantomime at the school. Come on, let's get ready.

You can have a lot of fun with pacing and leading as well as avoiding potentially confrontational situations. You will be surprised how easy it is to connect things in this way once you have practised the technique.

Fine-tune your senses for feedback

The communication process described above is greatly enhanced if you can learn to recognise the state changes discussed in the previous chapter in other people as well as yourself. This means sharpening up your senses so that you can spot changes in yourself and others that usually go unnoticed. In NLP this is called 'sensory acuity'. Without good sensory acuity, the effectiveness of any techniques you learn will be very limited indeed. How can you have any influence if you are unable to read the way people are communicating and feeling? You may passionately explain to people how your master plan is brilliant, but, if they think otherwise and you miss their signals of disbelief, then you have only convinced yourself!

> without good sensory acuity, the effectiveness of any techniques you learn will be very limited

To influence others, you need your senses to be tuned in to certain physiological signs that indicate whether they are with you or not. If you miss the unconscious signals people transmit via their body language and tone of voice, then you are ignorant of most of the message they are conveying.

What you want to do is realise when a person's state has changed and whether or not the state he or she is in is useful for the outcome you have in mind. If you are selling, you want your customer to be in a 'buying' state. If you are giving a presentation, you want your audience to be in a 'receptive' state. For example, when we run workshops, we make sure that we pace and lead our participants from whatever state they are in when they arrive to a 'curious to learn' state before getting into the first session. We can only do this if we have the sensory acuity to identify their initial states.

It makes sense to prepare yourself, and others, before engaging in a matter involving communication or even when just relaxing. Surprisingly few people intentionally prepare their state for what they want to achieve. It is easy to end up in an inappropriate state for all kinds of activities – for example, going to seminars in a 'you can't teach me anything' state or 'another boring seminar' state; going to work in a 'I hate Mondays' state or 'I'm not looking forward to the meeting' state; arriving home after a long day's work in a 'please don't ask me for anything' state or a 'the kids are making too much noise' state.

> few people intentionally prepare their state for what they want to achieve

Here are some of the outward signs to look for when trying to spot a state:

● voice characteristics (tone, speed, timbre, volume, flow)
● body posture
● tension in certain parts of the body
● breathing pattern
● lip size
● pupil size
● lines on the face
● skin colour.

Assessing these external indicators of internal states is called 'calibrating' a state. Think of it as taking a reading of a person's state.

Noticing and recording states for future reference

When you meet a person who tells you that he or she is feeling frustrated, that is the time to calibrate the state he or she is in by assessing all the aspects of the person's physiology listed above. As the person is in a 'frustrated' state, you are unlikely to get him or her to connect with your topic while this state exists. If you ever have to deal with that person again, you will know what signs to look for that show he or she is frustrated. If, say, the signals are screwing up the face, squeezing the fists and grinding the teeth, if you notice these, you can begin to pace and lead the person into a more receptive state, rather than dive straight in with your idea and have it rejected simply because the person is in the wrong state to consider it properly.

Some people are not easy to calibrate – typically, those who like to keep their emotions to themselves. They will test your skills of sensory acuity and calibration to the full. Look carefully for changes in their physiology – maybe a very slight change in posture or lip size, for example. The signs will be there as the body always shows a change of state.

To develop your sensory acuity, you will need to practise calibrating the physiology of people as they change between states. Avoid trying to interpret what any state means. If you say 'Jack looks depressed' you may be correct, but then again you really don't know unless Jack previously told you that he was depressed and his physiology at the time was the same as it is now. You can only truly interpret what a state means when the person has given you evidence that describes it.

Give people time to think

In any form of communication, people need time to think about what they are listening to and observing. They want to process information as it is received. While doing so, they have to stop listening – in NLP the term used for this is 'downtime'. Having the sensory acuity to notice when a person is processing in downtime is fundamental to building rapport, pacing and leading and, ultimately, effective communication. For example, during a conversation, if a person has his or her eyes open and directed your way, does it mean that the person is looking at you and listening? Could be, but, then again, if the eyes are glazed over or focused on a point somewhere in the distance, he or she is likely to be in downtime, thinking of something else. The senses of sight and hearing can be directed either inwards or outwards. When you are 'in your head', running images, conversations and other sounds that make up your thoughts, you will not be taking in any information from around you, regardless of where your eyes are looking. In order to be fully alert to your surroundings, your senses must be focused outwards. When you are in conversation with another person, you know if he or she is listening to you from the eye movements – roving eyes or a distant focus tell you that other thoughts are uppermost inside the person's head.

Reading eye patterns for useful information

> one of the biggest giveaways is the movement of the eyes

There are many aspects of physiology that give clues to how a person is thinking or feeling. One of the biggest giveaways is the movement of the eyes. Once you know what certain movements mean, you can determine how a person is accessing information and use this knowledge to influence them.

The eyes are considered to be windows to the soul. They also indicate the way a person is thinking. Because the eyes are hardwired to both sides of the brain, they move in accord with the thinking process. Unless you are a gifted mind-reader, you still will not be able to tell *what* a person is thinking, but, with a little practice, you will be able to tell *how* a person is thinking.

A thought can consist of visual, auditory and kinaesthetic information, which is revealed by the position of the eyes. Just think for a moment how you can use this information with people you want to influence. If you can tell whether people are thinking in pictures, sounds or feelings, just think how much more effectively you could communicate with them. Can you see how it would give you an angle on influencing them? Otherwise, the danger is that you miss the signals and totally mismatch their communication – for example, using a 'feeling mode' with someone who is processing in a 'visual mode'. This is a common and frequent cause of miscommunication between people and, at worst, can create conflict. Depending in which direction the eyes are looking, you can pick up the mode in which the person is thinking, as shown in the diagrams that follow, and avoid this problem.

Characteristics of communication modes

The following descriptions are valid for a right-handed person. Note that some left-handed people may be configured the opposite way around. While you read the descriptions below, keep in mind that we use all the modes of communication, but some people may rely on one dominant mode and use the other modes with far less frequency and clarity. Whichever mode is used most often, this will be the mode in which you are able to communicate most effectively.

Visual thinking mode

Upwards at any angle above the horizon is where the eyes go when you are accessing images. Up to the left indicates the recall of a visual memory and up to the right indicates a constructed image. Flicking from up-left to up-right and back again indicates that both recall and construction are taking place.

People who use the visual mode frequently in their communication often speak quickly and in a high pitch as they synchronise their voice with the images flashing through their minds. This process affects the breathing because, when you speak quickly, there isn't time to take in air all the way down to the lower abdomen, so you will notice the upper chest rising and falling.

Visual recall

In conversation, the visual communicator will have a tendency to choose visual words, such as:

● 'Can you *see* what I mean?'
● 'I'll *paint* you a *picture*.'
● 'It's *bright* and *clear*.'
● 'Let's *zoom in* on this.'

Visual construct

brilliant example

Tessa functioned at such a fast rate in the visual mode that she had 'forgotten' how to feel. She could see the solution to problems so quickly in her mind that she didn't stop to think about how she or anyone else felt about them. People had trouble keeping up with her and, consequently, her ability to communicate effectively was impaired. Over time, she had become severely stressed as a result and was having medical treatment for conditions that appeared to exist only in her mind.

On recognising this and after some practice, she was able to reconnect with her feelings. She went on to make some major changes in her life and is now a much happier, healthier person.

Auditory thinking mode

A lateral left movement of the eyes indicates a remembered sound, such as a conversation or piece of music. A lateral right movement indicates a constructed sound or conversation.

People who use the auditory mode frequently in their communication tend to speak with a varying tone. They are likely to breathe from the mid-chest area.

In conversation, the auditory communicator will have a tendency to choose auditory words, such as:

Auditory recall

- 'I *hear* what you say.'
- 'That *rings* a bell.'
- 'It *sounds* OK to me.'
- 'It's *music* to my ears.'

Auditory construct

▶ brilliant example

Paula lived with her elderly mother and was becoming increasingly frustrated about the amount of time her mother spent watching soaps on television. Paula functioned mainly via the auditory channel and couldn't understand the need for such visual stimulation. However, Paula would go about her daily jobs with her personal stereo plugged in, listening to *The Archers*. Both were interested in soaps, but preferred different channels.

With her newfound awareness of this, Paula was able to be a great deal more tolerant of her mother.

Internal dialogue thinking mode

When the eyes are down to the left, it indicates that an inner conversation is going on. We all have an internal voice that we use to talk with ourselves as we are thinking or run habitual loops of dialogue.

There is no characteristic breathing pattern accompanying this mode, but it is common for people who are in deep conversation with themselves to put a hand on the side of their face or stroke their chin. This is the classic pose of 'the thinker'. You may even see the jaw moving, as if words are being mimed.

Internal dialogue

▶ **brilliant** example

Betty believed that she had a learning difficulty as she struggled to remember anything from lessons she attended. She had always thought that this was due to a lack of intelligence and poor memory.

During a training course, she learned that her internal dialogue was really to blame. Each time the trainer asked Betty a question, he noticed, from the position of her eyes, how she had been engaged in her own internal dialogue and, therefore, had not been listening to what was going on in the sessions.

On realising this, she made a conscious effort to stay tuned in to the trainer and, over time, managed to tame her inner dialogue.

Kinaesthetic thinking mode

Eyes down to the right indicate that someone is immersed in a feeling.

A person in this mode is likely to be breathing from the lower abdomen area and speaking slowly, with gaps between the words. Sometimes the gaps will be

Kinaesthetic

long. The gaps are needed to allow time for feelings to form before committing a word or phrase to speech – it must feel right before it is said. The voice will be low-pitched.

In conversation, the kinaesthetic communicator will have a tendency to choose feeling words, such as:

- 'This just *feels* right.'
- 'Let's *run* with this idea for a while.'
- 'You had better *get your skates on*.'
- 'We're in for a *bumpy ride* over the next week or so.'
- 'Let's keep in *touch*.'
- 'I *get the hang* of this now.'

▶ brilliant example

Graham used his feelings to communicate almost exclusively. During conversations he would take such a long time to form an answer that the person he was talking to would move the conversation on before he could finish a sentence. This led Graham to believe that people weren't interested in what he had to say. As a consequence, he developed the habit of tailing off his sentences before coming to the end. This reinforced his belief because people not only had to wait for him to reply but couldn't hear the full sentence when he did.

Once Graham realised this, he was able to finish his sentences with the same emphasis he started them with and change his belief about people not being interested in him.

Using this knowledge to improve communication

Knowing the mode a person uses to communicate is very useful if you want to get on the same wavelength and make your communication as effortless and effective as possible.

Underlying this technique is the responsibility that *you* have for the communication process. Do not expect others to fit in with your style. Be flexibile and adapt and you will have greater powers of influence. So, if you are asking someone a question using the visual mode, such as 'How do you see this panning out?' and the reply 'I don't see anything' comes back, it could be that you have chosen the wrong communication mode for that person. If, using your sensory acuity, you notice that the other person is using the kinaesthetic mode, you could then modify your question to fit with this, saying 'How does this feel to you as it begins to unfold?', for example.

> by modifying just a small aspect of your communication in this way, you can have a significant influence on people

By modifying just a small aspect of your communication in this way, you can have a significant influence on people. It's not so much the content of what you are saying that ensures you make the connection but the way you say it. Applying what you have learned about the visual, auditory, internal dialogue and kinaesthetic modes of communication can have a big impact on how others respond to you.

brilliant tip

Building rapport is an elegant, sincere process. It can become very mechanical and obvious if you are not genuinely interested in the person with whom you are building rapport, so make sure that you use these techniques with integrity.

CHAPTER 6

The impact of words

In the previous chapter you learned how to pace and lead using the concept of chunks of information and how words are an effective tool for creating change. Your language is just the superficial expression of the structure of your experience, behind which lies your kaleidoscope of values and beliefs. In the same way that your thinking becomes habitual and forms unconscious patterns, so

> Is your language working for you or against you?

does your language. Your memory bank of language consists of stock phrases that you use repeatedly. These reinforce your thinking and a cycle is established. Is your language working for you or against you?

How to use high-level language for positive results

High-level language, or large-sized chunks of information, is vague. Consider the statement, 'kids nowadays don't care'. It is vague because it omits the details of which kids, which days, how they show they don't care and what they don't care about. A statement like this will have been formed as a result of the speaker applying his or her personal values and beliefs to experience. The danger is that the speaker will now seek further evidence to defend the statement and ignore anything to the contrary. Compare such a scenario with the same pattern used in a positive way – 'kids today are so creative', for example. Its vagueness begs the same questions as the previous statement, but the consequences are far more uplifting and empowering.

Both statements demonstrate the three ways in which the mind selects and attaches meaning to experiences for storing in the memory. The first is by *generalising*, as in 'kids'. The second is by *deleting*, as in how specifically they don't care or in what ways they are creative. The third way is by *distorting*, as in 'don't care' and 'so creative' – the observation being distorted to fit the perception of the speaker, to match what he or she has chosen to believe.

Milton Erickson was a highly effective and unconventional therapist. His methods were modelled by the originators of NLP in *Patterns of the Hypnotic Techniques of Milton H. Erickson, MD: Volume 1* and *Volume 2* by Richard Bandler and John Grinder (Metamorphous Press, 1996 and 1997). Milton used vague language to help people change the way they think. The language patterns he used became known as 'artfully vague' language. He used the patterns to help people change the way they represent their experiences internally, rather than give direct advice on what to do. Your personal perception of events is called your 'map of reality' and no two people's maps are alike.

Milton realised that his clients *wanted* to change, but making them defensive would not help. So, he agreed with whatever his clients presented as their map of reality, no matter how absurd it sounded. He then used language to make it easy for clients to create their own changes.

---

brilliant example

A sales executive wanted to improve his results, but was hesitant when talking to new prospects. The root of the hesitancy was an experience of a visit to a new prospect that didn't go well. The prospect ignored him and 'made him feel small' (his words). His memory of this event brought up the emotion of 'feeling small', which became a barrier to gaining new clients.

During the coaching he was questioned and offered statements that agreed with the way he was thinking. The manner in which the statements were delivered caused him to realise the absurdity of what he was doing to himself. One of the statements that created a big shift for him was, 'Wow! Isn't it incredible how you instinctively know that all new prospects are waiting for you to call on them so that they can make you feel small?' This statement agreed with his map of reality, yet emphasised the absurdity of it at the same time. There was nothing to defend or disagree with.

After coaching, he changed his perception of the negative experience and this allowed him to be confident about future visits to new prospects. As a result, his new client conversion rate increased significantly.

Think how often you use limiting language to yourself to determine what you can and can't do. Next time you hear yourself saying that you can't

think how often you use limiting language to yourself

do something you would like to do, just listen to your reasoning and ask yourself where such 'beliefs' – because that's what they are – have come from.

Here are some language patterns to look out for. If you find yourself using them in a positive way, then generate more. The examples here demonstrate patterns being used in a limiting way and include questions that help to create positive change.

Generalisation

The speaker takes a particular experience and applies it to a multitude of other situations. Let's look at some examples.

'You can't run a family and work full-time'

- *Questions* What can't you do? What stops you? What tells you that? Who can't? Do you know anyone who does? How many hours and days are you thinking of? What if you could?

- *Words to listen for* Can't, unable, not possible.

'Children need discipline'

- *Questions* Need? Which children? Discipline in what way? What else do they need? Who says?

- *Words to listen for* Need, must, have to, got to, necessary, requirement.

'Nobody loves me'

- *Questions* Nobody? Is there one person who does/doesn't? What tells you that? How are you measuring love? Do you love anyone?

- *Words to listen for* Everybody, nobody, anyone, every, always, never.

Deletion

Details are deleted as the speaker chooses what to focus on. Here are some examples.

'He's a failure'

- *Questions* How did he fail exactly? What did he fail at? Who says so? Has he failed at everything he's done? Is there nothing he has succeeded at? Has he not succeeded at drawing your attention? What else is he succeeding with?

- *Words to listen for* Instances where a verb has been turned into a noun, such as 'failing at' becomes 'failure' or 'he is performing' becomes 'his performance' or 'he is succeeding' becomes 'his success'.

'Her children are not very bright'
- *Questions* Compared to whom? What standard/who are you measuring them against? Bright in what way?
- *Words to listen for* Those that require an opposite, such as good, bad, cold, hot, bright, dull, sincere, insincere, happy, sad, rich, poor.

'She rejected me'
- *Questions* What did she do that you are calling rejection?
- *Words to listen for* Verbs that require clarification.

'They were left to fend for themselves'
- *Questions* Who are they? What do you mean by fend?
- *Words to listen for* Non-specific references to people/things such as they, people, computers, children.

Distortion

'He never buys me flowers so he doesn't love me'
- *Questions* In what way does him not buying you flowers mean that he doesn't love you? In what ways does he show that he loves you?
- Words/patterns to listen for – statements that don't 'add up', where a conclusion stated in the second part is based on the meaning attached in the first part.

'My children are driving me crazy'
- *Questions* What specifically are they doing to cause you to feel crazy? What are your children doing when you choose to go crazy?
- *Words and phrases to listen for* Statements in which one thing causes another.

'I know you don't want to support my initiative'

- *Questions* How do you know? What tells you that? You can read my mind?

- *Words and phrases to listen for* Statements that include conjecture and suggest mind-reading.

'Families should stick together through all life's challenges'

- *Questions* Who said that? Who are you quoting?

- *Words and phrases to listen for* Statements that lack reference to the author.

Using what we've learned

NLP calls the above 'metamodel' questions because they make us aware of the higher-level (meta) meaning of our words. They bring into conscious awareness the deep-rooted patterns of meaning that have been created out of our values and beliefs. All too often, negative vague language becomes part of the programming used in everyday life. You have seen how easy it is to develop beliefs that have a major impact on the way you behave. Your language is greatly influenced by your beliefs and associated values.

Artfully vague language patterns are positive and offer alternative choices in such a way that the individual is empowered to make whatever changes will help to bring about better-quality results. Think of the metamodel as an antidote to limiting vague language. It clarifies by getting to the specifics of an experience. It does this by questioning the generalisations, deletions and distortions that we have constructed.

When we break down language in this way, it's easy to see also how our thought patterns become demotivating and limiting – not only for ourselves but also for the people around us.

More insight into the way we use language can be gauged from the way we use the past, present and future tenses. You will often hear people say things such as:

- 'I will never be able to do that.'
- 'I can't go under water.'
- 'I'm not a team player.'
- 'I don't seem able to hold down a job.'
- 'I can't run for more than ten minutes.'
- 'My manager and I don't see eye to eye.'
- 'I'm no good at numbers.'
- 'If I tried that, I'd certainly fail.'

Note that all these statements are in the present tense – as a human being, you have an amazing capacity to carry past experiences with you in the here and now. Sometimes this is enjoyable – as when you recall pleasant memories and plan your future based on memorable experiences – but, when you apply the present tense to negative experiences, it can limit your potential. Your memories can be like old clothes. They

> when you apply the present tense to negative experiences, it can limit your potential

become unfashionable or worn out, but you can't bear to throw them away, so they hang in the wardrobe, taking up space and preventing your other clothes from looking fresh and smart.

The problem with the makers of the statements above is that the desire to change is overshadowed by the strength of the belief they carry. By changing the tense of statements, you can start to gently loosen the hold of the limiting belief. Here are some examples.

- 'I can't go under water' *becomes* 'In the past I have not felt comfortable going under water.'
- 'I'm not a team player' *becomes* 'My experience of working in teams to date has not been enjoyable.'
- 'I don't seem able to hold down a job' *becomes* 'Previously I have had some challenges settling into a job.'

- 'I can't run for more than ten minutes' *becomes* 'I can run for up to ten minutes.'

- 'My manager and I don't see eye to eye' *becomes* 'My manager and I have had one or two differences in the past.'

- 'I'm no good at numbers' *becomes* 'I have had a challenge or two with arithmetic.'

- 'I will never be able to do that' *becomes* 'Up until now I have not been able to achieve this.' (Notice also the subtle change from 'that' and a flat dismissal of the action, suggesting dissociation, to the positive attempt at making it work.)

- 'If I tried that, I'd certainly fail' *becomes* 'I have never tried it before, but I am willing to have a go.'

The last statement is interesting in that it is not even based on a past experience. It predicts failure and so prevents the speaker from trying something new.

Putting the statements into the past tense suggests that there is a *possibility* things can change now and in the future. To create a real change in behaviour, you have to work on designing the future. For that to happen, there has to be a real desire to bring it about. With a real desire to change, you can add the future intention. For example, a person with a real desire to build a relationship with his manager might say, 'In the past, my manager and I have had our differences, but I am going to make a real effort to listen and understand his point of view.'

Similarly, the person having difficulty with arithmetic but with a real desire to keep the household accounts in order might say, 'In the past, I have had some challenges with arithmetic, but I am going to take some lessons and practise adding up so that I can keep on top of my finances.'

We encourage you to listen closely to the words people say and to your own internal dialogue and challenge it where appropriate using the metamodel questions.

Using metaphors to create change

Further insight into the ways people think can be gained by observing what metaphors they use. Metaphors are also very effective tools when pacing and leading other people.

Some people have a way of using metaphors that gives away their map of reality. Some such patterns have become part of the everyday language we all use. Here are some common examples.

- It's like watching paint dry.
- She was like a bull in a china shop.
- This is the Rolls-Royce edition.
- It's like walking through treacle.
- We need to ride the storm.

Metaphors like these are a manifestation of a map of reality. Identifying with a person's metaphor can create instant rapport. You can pace and lead someone effectively and elegantly by picking up on their metaphors without even knowing the true content of their meaning. Here is an example from a conversation between David and Ben.

---

brilliant example

Ben: It's like the car is running, the wheels are going round, but we're not going anywhere.

David: Really! That must mean the engine's working very hard.

Ben: You're right, it is.

David: Then that must be putting a lot of strain on the engine.

Ben: You are absolutely right – it's like there is so much detail and I can't join up the dots.

David: Which dots?

Ben: The dots of my aspiration.

David: What do the dots look like?

Ben: I don't know – actually there aren't any.

In this conversation, David first joined Ben in his metaphor. He then led him from a state of frustration to a realisation that his stress was of his own making. Ben didn't know where his stress was coming from. By developing the metaphor, he became aware that the cause of his stress was an aspiration without a plan.

Persuading with elegance

It is easy to let words pass as the urgency to 'have your say' takes over. Every word can have an impact. Are your words having the impact you want?

> if you practise them, you will be able to influence and persuade elegantly

The aspects of language covered in this chapter give you options as to how you communicate. If you remember and practise them, you will be able to influence and persuade elegantly. Because language has such an immediate impact, you will find that your words will increase your personal power in such areas as:

- getting your ideas across
- coaching others
- working with groups
- presenting in public
- teaching
- negotiating

- parenting
- working through personal problems.

Above all, it will give you more confidence and positive energy in all areas of your life.

brilliant tip

The secret of effective questioning is to choose the one question that is absolutely appropriate to create a shift in someone's thinking. If we constantly ask questions just because we can, we will very soon become 'Billy no mates'.

CHAPTER 7

Debug the programmes you don't want

You have now covered all the main components that are involved in the way you communicate with yourself and others. The diagram below shows how NLP puts it all together. By generalising, deleting and distorting information, you create a state, that drives your behaviour. That is how your programmes are formed.

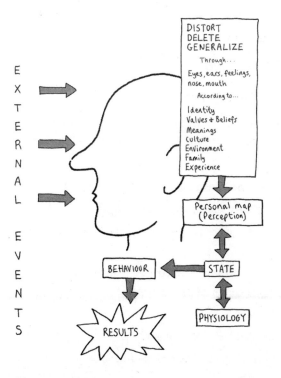

You have programmes for everything you do – motivating yourself, procrastinating, negotiating, getting tired, buying things. That includes all the things you would rather not do but continue with because you have formed a strong habit to do them. These programmes consist of sequences of thoughts and behaviour that are triggered by certain stimuli. In NLP, each sequence is called a 'strategy' for achieving an outcome. If you have ever tried to break a habit and failed, then it is more than likely that you were unaware of either the trigger or the unconscious parts of the strategy. Once you know about all the components of a strategy, you can do any number of things, including:

> once you know about all the components of a strategy, you can do any number of things

- changing it for something more useful
- copying an effective strategy from someone else
- designing a new one from scratch.

brilliant example

Dennis was very careful with his money. When he made a decision to buy something, he would follow a set strategy. It went something like this:

- visualise myself using it (internal visual)
- ask 'do I really need it?' (internal dialogue)
- if the answer is 'yes', research the model/type/make/price (internal visual)
- ask 'who shall I ask for an opinion?' (internal dialogue based on external reference metaprogramme)
- 'ask Jack and Bob' (external auditory)
- say 'yes, that feels right' (kinaesthetic)
- ask 'where shall I buy it from?' (internal dialogue)

- consider Internet/shop/mail order (internal visual)
- say 'yes, that feels right' (kinaesthetic)
- buy!

Compare this with Beverley's strategy:

- say 'that would look great on me' (external visual)
- try it on (external kinaesthetic)
- say 'looks good, feels good' (external visual and external kinaesthetic)
- buy!

Some people who are good at spelling use a strategy consisting of visual pictures of the letters placed in the correct order, usually brightly coloured. A common reason for some people not being good spellers is that they don't use such a good strategy. Poor spellers often try to spell by pronouncing words with their internal dialogue. Anyone can be a good speller – you just have to learn an effective strategy using visuals of words and not just what they sound like.

Ineffective strategies prevent people from achieving so many things. How well do you manage your finances? What about the presentations you have given? How well do you communicate with people at work? Are you a good cook? What about the way you make decisions? Can you maintain positive and fruitful relationships?

Whatever aspect of your life you want to improve, you can bet there is a strategy you are currently using that is holding you back, either creating inertia or producing undesirable results. The key is to know the beginning and end of each strategy so that you can change it.

Eliciting a strategy

When you elicit a strategy, you will discover values, beliefs and metaprogrammes plus a sequence of thoughts and behaviour.

Eliciting a strategy

Choose something you do that you would rather not do or something you would like to improve on – motivating yourself, stopping procrastinating, improving your decisionmaking or giving up smoking, for example.

Find the trigger

- How do you know when to do this?
- What lets you know you are ready to do this?
- What do you do as you are preparing to ... ?
- What steps do you go through?
- What happens next?
- Then what happens?
- How do you know when you have succeeded?
- How do you test whether or not you have succeeded?
- What lets you know that you have not yet succeeded?

Check the strategy

When you have elicited the complete strategy, repeat it back to check for anything missing. If you want to change it, the place to do this is at the trigger point. The object is not to remove the original strategy but to create an alternative choice, as the strategy may be useful in other contexts.

⚙ brilliant example

Norman wanted to stop smoking. He could manage without a cigarette most of the time, but found the urge irresistible when he had something to celebrate. At these times, his strategy included a visual of his hero on top of a mountain smoking a cigarette. This resulted in a strong belief that 'all successful people smoke', hence his need to smoke when he felt successful.

Once Norman realised that this was his trigger, he changed his belief to 'no matter how successful you are, smart people don't smoke'. He was then able to modify his strategy at the trigger point, removing the cigarette from his visual of his hero. As a consequence, he lost the urge to smoke.

Creating a new strategy

1   Think of a strategy that you would like to have. For example:

   - getting out of bed with a spring in your step
   - losing weight
   - keeping fit
   - arriving home after work feeling energetic
   - getting to sleep
   - doing your accounts
   - paying the bills
   - helping the children with their homework
   - improving your sports performance.

2   Create strong **values** and rock solid **beliefs** – stated in the positive – about the desire to have the strategy. For example, 'When I have this strategy, I will be able to do/have ...' or 'I really want this strategy because ...' and 'I can be/do ... whenever I choose to be/do ...'.

3   Decide on the trigger for your strategy. For example, if you want to lose weight, it could begin whenever the thought of food crosses your mind or it is time to prepare a meal or sit at the table.

4   Create a powerful series of images of you succeeding with the strategy. Break it down step by step, making each image big, bright and colourful. Keep the images dissociated and use strong, empowering internal dialogue.

5   Mentally practise your new strategy in slow motion as many times as it takes to programme your thinking.

6   Test the strategy by imagining a time in the future when you will want to use it. Run it through in your mind.

brilliant tip

When first working with strategies, there is a tendency to work with big chunks. The key to changing a strategy can lie in a quick internal visual or a belief change or in exaggerating or removing internal dialogue. Keeping to small chunks will allow you to access these finer details. Also, pay attention to the trigger point for a strategy – accessing the trigger point is vital to the strategy's success.

CHAPTER 8

Fantastic outcomes

Earlier, we introduced the five levels of alignment. We suggested that, for you to live a happy and fulfilled life, all the levels have to be aligned. What actually happens is that, no matter how well aligned you think you are, life has ways of enticing you to become misaligned. The decisions you make every day will either pull you closer to being aligned or push you further away from this

> no matter how well aligned you think you are, life has ways of enticing you to become misaligned

ideal. Sometimes, you can have all your levels lined up but still feel a tug. This can happen if your outcome is not clearly defined.

NLP has an approach to setting goals called 'well-formed outcomes'. For example, if you are about to make a difficult telephone call or apply for a new job or promotion, have you thought through the possible outcomes? What is your ideal outcome for attending the sales meeting next week? What is your intended outcome for spending time with your children? What is the outcome you would like to happen when you have that night out with your friends? What outcome are you aiming for with your new business idea, joining the squash club or taking up t'ai chi or yoga?

Once you have established a clear outcome, you can decide what role you will play, be able to establish your values and beliefs concerning the situation, develop your capabilities, adjust your behaviour and have a positive impact on your surroundings.

Do I need a purpose or an outcome?

Think of 'purpose' as being at a higher level than 'identity' – more about the essence of who you are than a description of your role.

brilliant example

Colin described his role as 'a life coach working with people to facilitate positive personal change'. He described his purpose as being 'to help people realise their true potential'. As he goes about his work as a life coach, Colin keeps this purpose at the forefront of his mind. However, the outcome he wants for each session will depend on the individual needs of his client.

A strong sense of purpose provides you with the energy to move forward with certainty and confidence. Outcomes focus on being clear about your desired results in specific situations.

> outcomes differ from goals ... by setting outcomes, there is so much more you can achieve

Outcomes differ from goals in that a goal usually takes the form of a short statement about what you want to achieve. An outcome considers other consequences of the effort applied to achieving the goal. When you merely state a goal, then that is what you measure. By setting outcomes, there is so much more you can achieve.

▶ **brilliant** example

Tim set a goal to increase new account sales by 15 per cent by the end of the quarter. His outcomes, as a result of having achieved the increase, were 'for his team to feel good about their contribution, the new clients to be happy with the service, potential for further added-value sales and the team to have learned more about selling and influencing.'

Making sure that your outcomes are well formed

The acronym PRIEST provides a framework for determining the strength and validity of any outcome to ensure that it is well formed.

P is for positively stated

A feature of the human mind is its inability to process a negative. Consider the instruction, 'Whatever you do, do *not* think about a pink elephant.' Oh! Too late, you thought about one didn't you? We know you did because you *have* to think of the thing you are not supposed to think about!

Beware of your capacity to 'get what you focus on'. If your main focus is on what you don't *want*, you may end up getting it. To avoid this, make

> beware of your capacity to 'get what you focus on'

sure that your outcomes are clearly stated in the positive. In other words, say what you *do* want, not what you *don't* want (a pink elephant).

R is for resources

This includes internal as well as external resources. Do you have the courage, confidence, staying power, commitment, determination and other internal resources you may need to succeed?

If not, there are NLP techniques you can use to acquire them. What external resources will you need – finance, people, knowledge?

I is for initiated and maintained by self

Is the achievement of the outcome totally in your control or does it depend on something outside your control?

You may want to adjust your outcome if you are not fully in control. Even if you have other people to help you, make sure that you keep hold of the responsibility for your choices – whether things go according to plan or not.

E is for ecology

Have you considered the consequences of achieving your outcome? What are the likely impacts on other people and other aspects of your life? Are they acceptable to you?

This is known as an 'ecology check'.

S is for sensory evidence

What sensory evidence will tell you that you have successfully achieved your outcomes? What will you hear? What will you see and how will you feel?

Take some time to imagine how things will be in the future, having achieved what you set out to achieve. How will you know that you have been successful?

T is for time

What timescale are you working to? How long will it take you to achieve all the outcomes attached to your goal?

If you write out your goals, it is very easy to miss something. The following exercise uses space and visualisation to help you set a realistic timescale and check how well formed your outcomes really are.

Visualise your success

Find a quiet space where you can visualise the journey of achievement. Mark a space on the floor to represent 'now'. From this space, walk to a point on the floor a particular distance away to represent the time you think it will take you to achieve your outcomes. Stand on this point and look back at 'now'. Spend some time feeling what it's like to have achieved all your outcomes.

Next, walk a little further into the future and turn around. Look back at 'now' again and visualise what you did to achieve your outcomes. Make sure that your internal language is in the past tense. Once your mind has grasped the idea that you have already succeeded, visualising what you *did* as opposed to what you *have to do* is a much more creative, insightful and far less stressful process. It's very powerful and great fun, too.

▶ brilliant example

Linda likes to look after people and entertain. Her outcome for a night out was to make sure that Joy enjoyed her birthday after a period of illness (positively stated). She booked Joy's favourite restaurant, made sure all the guests were happy to contribute to the event, took responsibility (initiated by self) for making sure that the guests knew the location, where to park and gave them an arrival time and a dress code (internal and external resources). She checked that Joy's health was up to such a night (ecology). Linda created an image in her mind of the guests leaving the restaurant smiling and laughing and Joy sitting happily at the table having had a wonderful evening (sensory-based evidence).

The schedule of things to do before the event helped it run smoothly and allowed Linda to enjoy the evening as much as Joy (timing). A hostess with real purpose and drive!

Consider what the consequences of not having well-formed outcomes to achieve her goal would have been. She might have left preparations to the last minute, found Joy's favourite restaurant to be fully booked, spent the hours before the event taking phone calls from guests needing directions, felt bad and had to apologise to Joy for not having booked her favourite restaurant and arrived in a flustered state, unable to give Joy and the guests her attention.

How well everyday experiences like this go make a big difference to your energy and results. Taking the PRIEST approach helps with the present and opens up future possibilities. Linda's reputation for organising events calmly and effectively is a skill that she can apply to other areas of her life, including her work and family. When you work with outcomes in this way, you generate positive energy that will attract positive people to you.

brilliant example

Despite an underprivileged upbringing, Tom has an unstoppable sense of purpose. Combining his skills as an expressive dancer with his ability to teach dance as a way of helping youngsters to be confident and believe in themselves, he embarked on a mission.

When we met Tom, he had a very clear outcome in mind: he wanted to establish a dancing competition that enabled teams from schools around London to choreograph and perform their own dance creations. They would then enter a series of qualifying events and the teams chosen for the final would have the opportunity to dance on stage at Olympia.

Tom took on the role of organiser and his values concerning the young people and creative expression held him in good stead. He worked on his self-belief and quickly acquired the internal resources of confidence and determination he needed to turn the idea into a series of actions. From there on, he knew where to find the external resources he needed and took control of the entire project. Tom knew exactly what he would hear, see and feel when the event was successful.

Six months later, hundreds of highly expressive youngsters took to the stage at the first Olympiada ever in the UK. It was a great success.

Putting everything together to create a brilliant future

If you have followed all the exercises in this book you now have everything you need to create a brilliant future for yourself.

The next exercise gives you a structure for choosing which techniques are appropriate to make the desired changes. It can be used in conjunction with the PRIEST exercise or on its own as a way of becoming aligned with a personal change you want to make. It is used here along with the PRIEST exercise. As you proceed, there are suggested techniques you may wish to use, some of which you have covered in previous sections of the book, while others are in Chapter 10.

Creating a brilliant future

1 Prepare a set of cards or sheets of paper marked as follows.

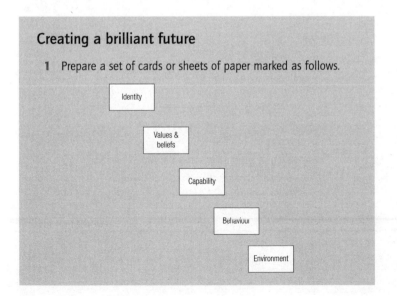

2 Sit in a quiet place, relax and look up. Create an image of what life will be like at some point in the future. Choose a period when you have achieved one or more of the outcomes that are important to you now.

3 Mark two spots on the floor – one to represent today and one for a time in the future when you will have achieved a specific outcome. The distance (time) between the two spots should be what feels right. Stand on the future spot and imagine what it is like. Imagine you have a remote control like the one you use for your television. Use it to intensify the qualities of your internal imagery and sound. Turn up the brightness, increase the colour, improve the contrast, make it bigger and bring it closer. Turn up the volume and listen to the sounds. Have the sound well tuned so there is no interference. Step into the picture and notice the feelings of satisfaction and achievement. Enjoy the moment and anchor this state.

Technique used

● Anchoring

4 Lay the cards you made above, in the same order, at equal intervals between where you are standing now ('future') and the spot representing 'today'.

5 Stand at a point just beyond the 'future' spot and look back at 'today'. Fire the anchor you set earlier. How does it feel, having achieved your outcome(s)? From this position, what have you got to say to the you of 'today'? Have you any tips or advice?

6 Move to the 'Identity' card. Ask yourself how you have changed, now that you have achieved your outcome(s). What is different about you? What role are you now playing that you were not playing before?

7 Move to the 'Values & beliefs' card. What values have you changed, if any, and how have your beliefs changed in order to achieve this success?

Techniques used

- Values elicitation
- Belief change
- Reframing
- This not that
- Metamodel.

8   Move to the 'Capability' spot. How have your capabilities changed? What did you learn along the way?

Techniques used

- Artfully vague language.

9   Move to the 'Behaviour' card. What did you do along the way? What are you doing differently now?

Techniques used

- New behaviour generator (in Chapter 10)
- Collapsing anchors
- Anchoring
- PRIEST
- Strategies.

10 Move on to the 'Environment' card. What impact has achieving your outcome(s) had on those around you? Is your environment still the same or has it changed at all? If so, how?

Technique used

- Perceptual positions (in Chapter 10)

11 Revisit the cards in any order you wish if you feel that there is still work to do. You will know when you have true alignment as, then, all the tugs will have disappeared and you will have a burning desire to make your first move.

Spacing the cards out on the floor helps you to 'programme in' the changes you want to make and gives you a better concept of space and time than if you just did the exercise mentally. If you have completed the exercise correctly, there is no need to write anything down – you will then have integrated it firmly and clearly.

brilliant tip

Begin thinking about future goals as if you have already achieved them. Ask yourself what the outcomes were. Try this with, for example, making a telephone call, going to a meeting, having a touchy conversation with your partner, buying a new house or car. Assume that the event has passed and you were successful. What have been the outcomes? What have you achieved? Make the answers to these questions your focus as you work towards achieving them for real.

CHAPTER 9

Adopting the beliefs on which NLP is based

Now that you have some experience of NLP, adopting the beliefs on which it is founded will expedite your journey to success. NLP was originally used to model excellence. The following beliefs were modelled from people who excelled in their field. They are referred to as the 'presuppositions' of NLP.

The map is not the territory

You have your own unique understanding of the world around you. Whatever your perception is, it isn't how it actually is! You can never have *all* the information *all* the time. Just as a map doesn't show every house, shop, tree or bump in the road, your map is merely your representation of the world rather than reality.

---

brilliant example

Sue and Sam went shopping at the same supermarket at the same time.

Sam would shop intuitively, without even a list, but for Sue, shopping was like a military campaign. She took a list of what she needed, worked out an efficient route through the aisles and bought only what was on the list. Sue could never quite understand how Sam would wander around the supermarket aimlessly choosing items he fancied, while Sam would make fun of Sue's regimented precision.

You create your map by filtering information through your senses, the language you use, your beliefs and values, and your experience.

Respect others' maps of the world

Developing a state of curiosity is one of the most useful states you can achieve if you are going to communicate successfully. If everyone's map is different, who is to say who has the right one or the best one? An effective state of curiosity will allow you to gain information about the other person's map, which will help you to build rapport, as well as communicate with and influence them. An effective state of curiosity includes a healthy respect for other people's maps. It does not mean that you have to agree, but it is useful to understand them.

▶ brilliant example

Ingrid's map differed from her son Greg's.

His mother away for the weekend, Greg decided to invite his friends round for a party. Things got out of hand and considerable damage ensued.

Greg was very apologetic, thus respecting Ingrid's map, and Ingrid respected Greg's desire to have teenage fun. Together they were able to work out a plan to get the house put right.

The meaning of your communication is the response you get

Taking responsibility for your communication will give you control over the process and the results. It is common for people to give their view of something and then blame others or circumstances when they are not understood.

If you want control over your success, then take responsibility for your communication. If you don't get the response you expected first time, then try explaining things differently.

> if you want control over your success, then take responsibility for your communication

brilliant example

Harry was passionate about his new idea and used all the expressive body language he could muster to explain it to Tara. Tara sat, hardly moving, as she listened intently. Harry, however, interpreted this as 'Tara is not interested'.

If it's possible for one person, it's possible for others

You have all the resources you need to make changes in your life. In situations where you find yourself struggling to achieve, it's not that you don't have the internal resources, it's just that you are in an unresourceful state.

> you have all the resources you need to make changes in your life

Developing resourceful states is crucial to the pursuit of success. You can achieve anything you decide, but some things will take longer than others. Be sure to check the consequences of dedicating your life to achieving your aspirations.

brilliant example

Years ago, doctors believed that if you ran fast enough to complete a mile within four minutes your heart would stop – until Roger Bannister did it. No sooner had Roger achieved the four-minute mile than his record was broken over and over again by other athletes who had had their belief changed.

There is no failure, only feedback

If what you do isn't creating the desired result, you have still created *a* result. Use the feedback you receive to explore what you can do differently to get the outcome you want. Ask yourself, 'What can I learn from this?' and 'What can I do differently?'

focus on solutions not on problems

Focus on solutions and what else is possible, not on problems. Failure exists only as a state of mind – a perception.

brilliant example

Niall Fitzgerald worked for Unilever in the early 1990s and was responsible for launching Persil Power. It had to be recalled after being on supermarket shelves for only one day because it was too powerful – it destroyed clothes. Unilever's board figured that the learning process had been worth the huge financial cost invested as it provided valuable feedback for the next project.

Niall Fitzgerald was promoted to UK chairman in 1996.

Mind and body are part of the same system

The way you think has a direct impact on your physiology. If your thoughts are making you feel sad, then your body will reflect this. If your thoughts are making you feel happy, then your body will reflect this, too. Negative thinking has a tendency to cause stress and tension, blocking energy flow. Indeed, it is increasingly recognised that serious illnesses can be caused by the build-up of stress. Clearly, it makes sense to keep energy flowing by thinking positively.

brilliant example

Watch any sportsmen and women at the top of their game and you will see how they think their way to success. They do it by generating a positive belief and state of control followed by consistent practice.

Every behaviour has a positive intention

You make the best choices you can with the resources you have available at the time. The intention relating to your choice is a positive one for you, even though others may not see it that way.

brilliant example

Ben chose not to telephone a girl he met at a party the previous evening, even though they had got on really well and she had been delighted when he asked for her telephone number. Past experience of relationships with girls told Ben that he would get hurt. His behaviour reflected his positive intention to protect himself from perceived future hurt, but the girl was disappointed when he didn't call.

The person with the most flexibility will control the system

Flexibility in relation to thinking and behaviour will give you the advantage when it comes to understanding other people's maps of reality, building rapport and achieving outcomes. Being too fixed and rigid can create a stalemate situation, with no desired outcomes being achieved, and can also restrict the number of people you can build rapport with.

Flexibility does not mean giving way to every idea, but, rather, being able to adapt and pace and lead with your thinking and behaviour. Inflexibility is narrow-mindedness, having fixed ideas and 'one way of doing things'.

brilliant example

Janine wondered why she hadn't been promoted. She had been with her company in the same role for a number of years and had watched people come into the organisation and receive promotion before her. She did her job well but hadn't realised that she 'chose' who to associate with on the basis of those she got on well with and inadvertently alienated everyone else.

Promotion came easily once she learned to flex her behaviour to achieve her well-formed outcomes.

If you always do what you've always done, you'll always get what you've always had

> until you reprogramme your thinking, your results are unlikely to change

Unconscious programming causes you to repeat patterns, even though you are aware that they are not working. Until you learn to reprogramme your thinking, your results are unlikely to change.

brilliant example

Brian had been married three times and had had a number of other unsuccessful relationships.

He blamed the women in his life for his inability to make the relationships last. Unfortunately, he approached every relationship in the same way, making no changes to his thinking and behaviour, but expecting his partners to make changes to accommodate him. Once he became aware that he did this, he was able to make changes that involved respecting his partner's map.

Your behaviour is not who you are

Behaviour is something you do that is given meaning by other people. In other words, people make their own interpretations of your behaviour by using their own maps. Chances are that their interpretations are usually inaccurate. Successful people remember to look beyond behaviour in their interactions with others.

> successful people remember to look beyond behaviour

brilliant example

Thomas had spent a number of years in the Navy.

He had lied about his age and was accepted before he was 16. He had to harden up quickly and took a lot of abuse from his contemporaries. Consequently, he shaved his head, wore an earring and underwent weight training.

When Thomas eventually left the Navy, he still had the strong man appearance he had needed in the service for his own protection. Underneath, though, he was a passionate, creative man with some exceptional ideas for business.

Your perception is your reality

Your map of reality is created by the way you perceive things. Your perception of a situation will be different from that of, say, your next-door neighbour or your partner, offspring, manager or colleague.

On the basis that no two people can possibly have exactly the same experience, there are very few universal truths.

⟩ brilliant example

Rob became irritated because his girlfriend was consistently late for dates. He felt that she didn't love and respect him and became angry whenever they were together.

Fiona didn't place such a high value on time as Rob and found it hard to stick to a timetable. Her meetings with Rob were becoming increasingly unpleasant as he was invariably in a bad temper. She confided to her friend that she wanted to finish the relationship and find someone who was more fun to be with.

You are in charge of your mind and, therefore, your results

Everything starts with one thought. If you are in control of your thoughts, you are in control of your behaviour and, therefore, your results.

▶ **brilliant** example

Talking to Hannah the other day, it became clear that she was limiting her results with her narrow way of thinking. She consistently used language such as, 'I can't see that ever happening', 'It would be all right if only . . .', 'They [the management] will never allow that to happen'.

Spending her time thinking about what wasn't possible was leaving Hannah bereft when it came to finding solutions.

Resistance is a sign of a lack of rapport

After you have taken the trouble to build rapport with someone, you can lead and pace them to a win–win outcome. When rapport is absent, there will be signs of resistance – he or she will carry on with an activity while you are talking or there will be mismatches in your body postures. Without rapport, win–win outcomes are unlikely to be achieved.

▶ **brilliant** example

Liam doesn't like 'small talk'. He is a young man bursting with ideas, but lacks the finesse to get them across.

We taught Liam that 'small talk' is actually 'very big talk'. Without rapport, communication becomes strained and then ideas are often never aired.

You cannot not communicate

In the 1960s, Professor Albert Mehrabian conducted some research into the effectiveness of spoken communication. It resulted in the following statistics:

- 7 per cent of meaning is in the words that are spoken
- 38 per cent of meaning is in the way the words are said
- 55 per cent of meaning is in body language and facial expression.

Although these statistics are approximate – and are distorted when the telephone is being used – they highlight the importance of facial expression, body language and tone of voice in the communication process. Whatever you do, even if you think you are sitting quietly minding your own business, someone will be attaching meaning to your behaviour.

> whatever you do, someone will be attaching meaning to your behaviour

 brilliant example

Clegg sat with his arms folded throughout the meeting, saying nothing and every now and then letting out a large sigh.

People perceived him as being bored and disinterested. In reality, he was comfortable and listening intently, but suffering from a nasal problem.

You have all the resources you need to change

Believing this will help you to help yourself and others find the resources you need to make changes that serve you well.

 brilliant example

Debbie revealed to us that she didn't have a very long attention span. It transpired that she had been told this by a well-meaning geography teacher at school who really meant, 'You are not paying attention at this moment to the subject I am teaching you.' Debbie, though had carried this with her ever since, believing that she couldn't sit still in a whole variety of scenarios.

When we pointed out that Debbie *could* sit very still, focus when watching a film and for long periods when reading books by her favourite author, it was a simple process to draw out the resources she already had in one situation and apply them to another.

brilliant tip

In order to test your alignment with the underlying principles of NLP, ask yourself these two questions regarding each one.

1   What would happen if I lived by these principles?
2   What would happen if I lived by the opposite of each of these principles?

CHAPTER 10

A compendium of additional NLP techniques

Perceptual positions

Use this technique to understand other people's maps of reality and reach mutually beneficial agreements. For example, when preparing for meetings, dealing with family members, including children, in customer care, selling, negotiating, coaching and giving presentations.

When rapport is low and you are not getting along with someone you want to influence, it helps if you can see the relationship from the other person's point of view. The ability to look at an issue from a number of different perspectives can greatly add to the amount of information you have and help you to make better decisions and choices.

Seeing things from others' perspectives is a great start, but to hear and feel things from their perspectives as well is even more useful. By acting as if you are someone else you can begin to understand some of their beliefs, values and representations and gain a more complete understanding of how they might behave and react to the things you say and do. It enables you to understand others more and expand your own level of awareness.

The following exercise is designed to help you to gain a perspective on any given situation from three angles.

1   Think of a situation that you are going to face in the near future – one causing you some anxiety or apprehension.

2   You are going to view the situation from three different angles. Set a scene as though you are getting ready for a play, using props such as chairs and tables.

3   *First position – you* In this position, consider things only from your own point of view. You want to know how things affect you and how you feel. This first position is really useful when you want to assert yourself, check out how you feel about a situation or outcome and ensure that your needs are met. Staying here all the time, however, is unhelpful as you will have little, or no, awareness of your impact on others or their needs and preferences. You may also jump to conclusions without fully checking them out.

4   *Second position – the other person's shoes* Physically put yourself in the position of the other person in your scene. From here you can look back at yourself in the first position, step in to the other person's shoes and experience things the way they do. This is more than thinking about what you would do if you were them. It is about projecting 'you' into 'him or her' and really understanding the other person's perspective to gain more accurate information. What are his or her priorities? What pressure is he or she under? What values and beliefs are driving the person's behaviour? Adopting this position gives you a better understanding of the other person's behaviour and map of reality and, consequently, how he or she perceives you.

5   *Third position – fly on the wall* Now stand away from the scene so that you can see yourself in the first position and the other person in the second. From here, take on the role of an independent observer, detached and dissociated from the other two positions. Imagine you are a film director or a fly-on-the-wall documentary producer. You are observing from a logical,

rational and objective perspective. In this position you may notice what both parties can do differently to improve the relationship and achieve a win–win outcome.

6 Revisit any of the above positions to gain further understanding.

All three positions are equally valuable. By carrying out this exercise in real space and time, you can increase your understanding, your chances of building better rapport, create new ideas and solutions and open up new ways of thinking.

The swish technique

Use this technique to change a habit – for example, biting your nails, picking at skin, clock-watching, poor performance in sport, road rage, eating habits (identify specific triggers such as comfort eating or excitement). You can also use it to change your response to something, such as from 'immediate' to 'considered', or 'aggressive' to 'assertive'.

1   Choose a past negative situation where you demonstrated the
    behaviour you want to change. Create a fully associated image
    in your mind. Focus on what happened. Put a frame around the
    image. Identify one or two qualities of your internal image that,
    when intensified, change your internal response – you will
    probably notice this change as a feeling. Usually the brightness
    and size work best, but colour, contrast, location or depth may
    work also. Play around with this until you are happy with the
    chosen qualities.

2   Change your state by taking some deep breaths and stretching.

3   Create an image in your mind of the behaviour you would like
    to have instead. Really see yourself doing it. Make your picture
    dissociated – you are looking at yourself in the picture.
    Dissociated pictures create the motivation for moving towards
    something you want. Include all the resources you will need –
    strength, confidence, clarity of thought, listening ability,
    creativity, focus, relaxation, humour. Make your image
    compelling and realistic and check it out with respect to other
    areas of your life. Try it out with different contexts – is this 'new
    you' ecological with other relationships? If you were to respond
    in this way in different contexts, would the outcome be
    favourable to you and those you interact with? You may want to
    alter the image so that you are completely happy with it. When
    you are, intensify it and make it really compelling.

4   Shrink this image down to the size of a postage stamp,
    allowing the colour to drain out of it and all the sounds to
    become dull and muted.

5   Change your state.

6   Take your first image and increase the two strongest qualities
    you chose in step 1. Next, take your new self-image that you
    have shrunk and put it in the bottom corner of your first image.
    The next step should be done quickly. Say to yourself 'swish'

and, instantaneously, make the large picture small and dark, while making the new self-image large and bright. Make them swap places instantly and the negative image disappear completely.

Swish Technique

7 Repeat step 6 about five times, making sure that you change your state by taking some deep breaths and stretching between each one. Speed and repetition are essential.

8 Test your new response by imagining a time in the future when you will want this different response. This is called 'future pacing'. If you still get the original response, go back to step 1 and repeat the exercise. You will know when you have been successful because you will no longer be able to bring back the negative image.

New behaviour generator

Use this technique to create an entirely new behaviour.

1   With your eyes down to the left, ask yourself, 'If I were able to . . . (state your goal), what would I look like?'

2   With eyes up to the right, construct a visual image of what you would look like if you were in the act of achieving your goal. Construct the image from a dissociated point of view.

3   Mentally step inside the image so that you now feel yourself doing what you just saw yourself doing in the image. What do you see, hear and feel?

4   Compare the feelings you have with the feelings from a similar experience in which you were successful.

5   If the two feelings match, then you have finished.

6   If the two feelings don't match, then name what is missing – creativity, more confidence, being more relaxed and so on.

7   Refine your goal statement by adding 'and . . . (name the additional resource(s) you have chosen)'.

8   Go back to step 1 and repeat the exercise.

Visual squash

Use this technique to resolve conflicting beliefs or values in yourself. The trigger here is generally when you hear yourself saying 'Part of me wants to do/believes X and part of me wants to do/believes Y.'

1   Identify conflicting beliefs or wants.

2   Create a visual representation of each part, one in each hand, and hold them out in front of you.

3   Identify an outcome and ask for agreement from both parts.

4   Ask each part for its positive intention and continue chunking up to high-level values until you reach agreement.

5   Have each part look at the other and say what it sees and thinks. Include resources, strengths, beliefs and expectations.

6   Ask both parts to state their readiness to give and receive resources or negotiate if necessary.

7   Bring both hands together and pull both parts inside you to integrate them within you. They should do so willingly.

8   Check for objections from any other parts. If there are any objections, then do the exercise again with the objecting part present. Put this new part on a chair where you can relate to it from a distance.

Focus

If you find that, when doing certain activities, you are easily distracted, this technique will be very useful.

We bet that in some circumstances you are able to focus very well. It may be when you are watching a favourite television programme, shopping, enjoying a night out with friends, cutting your fingernails, shaving, combing your hair or reading a book you really enjoy. It's important to recognise it is not 'all the time' that you are unable to focus, which means you can spread this ability to other activities.

So, having identified an activity where you tend to lose focus and are easily distracted, ask yourself if it is of any value to you. What do you get from it? If you chose not to do it, what would the consequences be? Connecting with the outcome of any task will help you to engage fully with it; you will have a stronger purpose for doing it and doing it well.

Even when you are clear about the outcome of a task, however, and can see positive benefits for getting it done, the act of doing it may present a hurdle for you. It may be that, when you think of doing the task, you lose heart in it and lack the motivation to get started. If only you could get started. If you force yourself while being reluctant, though, you have forces working against you. Part of you wants to have the benefit that comes with completion and the other wishes you didn't have to do the task at all. When you approach anything in this frame of mind, and in this state, you have set yourself up to be easily distracted.

So, here's what you do. Recognise the feeling of avoidance. Where is the emotional tug coming from? Tell yourself that your state of avoidance is not serving you well and you really do want the benefit of having the task done. Visualise having the task done. Turn up the brightness, contrast and colour. Make sure you are projecting your mental image of task completion above the horizon level, intensify the image qualities even further and notice the feeling of satisfaction you have created.

Now, keep hold of this feeling and relax your breathing. Let go of any tension around your eyes, jaw and shoulders and gaze into the palm of your hand. Tell yourself that you are going to focus so much that wild horses will not be able to distract you – and neither will any other external sound, ringing phone, new e-mail, door closing, children shouting or traffic driving by. As you look into your palm, observe the detail on the surface of the skin. Look into the smallest crease and see how the lines join. Then look below the surface of the skin at the different colours – shades of red, yellow, blue. How many different shades of colour can you notice? After doing this for one minute, your attention will be highly focused. So now, keeping the same state of mind and with a clear, positive intention to do a job well, move your focus from your hand to the task before you and get on with it!

Image mapping

This technique is very fast and can be used to transfer internal resources, such as confidence, patience, humour, focus and decisiveness, from one context to another. It uses internal imagery – a little like the Swish technique but more subtle – to give you new options in situations where you have been experiencing difficulty. Use this technique when you may want a particular resource in more than one situation.

It is surprising how precise your mental imagery is in relation to your state of mind. So, for example, whenever you are feeling a certain way – perhaps anxious or frustrated – you will recreate the exact same imagery, internal dialogue and feelings that have become habitual in certain situations. So precise will this habit be that your mental imagery will always be in the same location, the same size, brightness and contrast as well as colour or black and white. You can test this by catching yourself in any mood and noticing your mental imagery. Do the same the next time you are in the same mood and check – your imagery will be identical. We can use this knowledge to create a lasting state change.

Habits are so powerful. The moment you have received a communication from someone, you will be firing a habitual response – click, click, click. There is little time to check what you are doing and make an alternative choice. Habits are hard-wired in. This technique allows you to choose to revisit one of these moments and, instead of responding in the usual way, remain resourceful and poised.

This is how you do it.

1 Recall a time when you reacted negatively to a person or situation.

2 Pay attention to the following aspects of your internal imagery.

- Location – where are you projecting this image precisely?

- Size – what shape is it and what size?

- Is it colour or black and white?

- Is there any sound with this image? If so, describe the audio qualities.

- How clear is the image? How bright is it?

3 Now, break this state by taking a very deep breath and adjusting your posture.

4 Decide what state you would like to replace the habitual one with. Let's call this state X.

5 Recall a situation when you had a strong experience of being in state X. The strength or intensity of the state is important. Make sure you choose a powerful state, not a weak one.

6 Pay attention to the aspects of your internal imagery attached to this experience described in step 2.

7 Now, retrieve your first image and move it so that it maps over the second more resourceful image associated with state X. The picture will remain the same, but take on the aspects of image X.

Job done. Now, try to get back the first image in its original location and you will find that it doesn't want to appear there any more. It will automatically shift to the new location with the new aspects and you will feel much more resourceful.

Image mapping can be used for many different states. I encourage you to play with it and explore the many resourceful states you can create for yourself for any context in which you want to feel more in control.

The wall of concentration

This is a very useful technique to enable you to maintain your concentration in a noisy environment. We have taught this technique to children who find it difficult to concentrate on their work because of the noise level in their classrooms.

1   Imagine that you have a soundproof frosted glass wall around you. Everything is still happening around you, but the sound is muted and you can only see hazy images through the glass.

2   You can develop the technique further by:
  ● imagining yourself pulling the glass up and down as and when you need it
  ● creating a noticeboard on the glass on which you can place sticky notes to remind yourself of things to do later
  ● installing a thermostat so that you can control the temperature while you are concentrating.

Once you know how your mind works, there are infinite possibilities for making this technique work positively for you.

Inner dialogue control

Sometimes what we say to ourselves isn't useful. Your inner voice may be giving you messages that limit you. Try some of the following techniques to switch off unhelpful internal dialogue.

1   Imagine that you have a volume control – turn it down so that you can no longer hear it.

2   Look up – it's almost impossible to talk to yourself with your eyes looking in this direction.

3   Turn the voice into a cartoon character.

4   Turn up the speed so that it sounds like a chipmunk.

5   Turn down the speed so that it sounds very deep and ridiculous.

brilliant tip

Once you have mastered a number of NLP techniques, be creative with them. Mix and match techniques for maximum impact. For example, while running a Perceptual Positions exercise, described at the beginning of this chapter, you could introduce a visualisation or a belief change or even a Swish or a Visual squash.

Conclusion

NLP is a skill that requires practice and your journey through this book is the first step towards a better life using what you have learned. We trust that you have enjoyed it and encourage you to continue practising the techniques you found most useful on a daily basis. As a result of practice, you develop confidence and, over time, new ways of thinking and behaving will come to you naturally.

Remember, being stuck with programmes that are limiting you is your choice. NLP gives you tools that make it easy for you to exercise more choice about the way you experience life. Choose well.

How to contact the authors

David Molden: david@quadrant1.com

Pat Hutchinson: pat@quadrant1.com

Website: **www.quadrant1.com**

---

brilliant questions and answers

Q Is all NLP training the same?

A The core skills of NLP are taught on most NLP courses. Beyond these core skills, the application of them tends to be split between those wanting to use NLP in their role as therapists and counsellors and those wanting to use NLP for themselves in business. NLP lends itself to both very effectively. Some courses run for 20 days over a period of 6 months, while others condense the learning into one block of around 7 to 9 days. Some courses attract large numbers of people; others restrict their participants to smaller group sizes of between 6 and 24 and offer a higher level of support and facilitation. There is no one standard, just many different formats.

Q **What does an NLP qualification do for me?**

A The value of NLP is not in the qualification, but in using it. We know lots of people who call themselves practitioners because they have attended a course and received a certificate. However, not every practitioner has integrated the skills. It depends how they have been taught. A true practitioner doesn't need to tell you that he or she has a certificate, but demonstrates his or her skills by achieving well-formed outcomes elegantly and ecologically. A certificate only shows that someone has attended a course – nothing more.

Q **How do I apply NLP to my everyday life?**

A Take it one step at a time. When you feel a tug, describe what was happening, without making a judgement. Avoid saying, 'He made me feel bad' or 'They won't listen to me'. Just describe what you noticed, such as, 'He put on a face and I felt uncertain and anxious'. Then refer to the book and decide which technique to use for that specific experience. Keep using it and it will become easier.

Q **What is the best way to learn NLP?**

A Our advice is to learn in a small group where you will receive expert tuition. During the learning process, many small nuances may be missed as two learners take turns playing the explorer and the facilitator. Access to experienced trainers at this stage is key if learners are to maximise their potential. From then on, it's practice, practice and more practice.

Take one aspect, such as eye position cues, and spend a whole week noticing how people move their eyes and what this suggests about how they are thinking (not *what* they are thinking – that would be an interpretation). The next week, practise matching and mirroring body language, then, the week after that, listen to voice tone, and so on. After a while, you will begin to do these things automatically. The more you practise, the easier it will become.

Q **I get the impression that NLP is like an exclusive club. I meet people who speak NLP jargon that I don't understand. Can you explain this?**

A Such people are not demonstrating their skills – they are showing off. Good practitioners make you feel comfortable in their company and show a genuine interest in you without talking in jargon.

Q **I have heard that NLP is manipulative. Is that true?**

A A knife can be used to manipulate someone to hand over all his or her valuables. It can also be used to manipulate a stone from a cherry. Like any tool or weapon, it's the intention of the person using it that's important. If something can be used to manipulate, does that mean we must view it with a negative mind? What about the knives and forks in your kitchen drawer? Act on what you know, not on what you hear people say.

Q **I have heard that there is no scientific evidence for NLP. Is that true?**

A NLP has pulled together the works of a number of eminent therapists, researchers and linguists. Bandler and Grinder studied the works of Alfred Korzybski, Milton Erikson, Virginia Satir and Fritz Pearls, to name but a few, and were encouraged by Gregory Bateson. Just Google these names if you want to trace the roots of NLP and read the early books by Bandler and Grinder.

NLP is eclectic. It draws from many disciplines that have their models and techniques grounded in both science and empirical evidence (see *Roots of Neurolingnistic Programming* by Robert Dilts, Metamorphous Press, 1989). Of course, like anything new, there are always people who feel threatened by NLP and seek to put it down in favour of their own pet theories. Remember that Galileo was imprisoned for showing evidence that the Earth revolved around the Sun. It took over a generation before his theory was accepted by the majority. The only real way to find out if NLP works is to try it for yourself.